96 Rules & Guidelines for the Professional Programmer

David Pankhurst

www.UtopiaMechanicus.com

To Gwen

Table of Contents

Forward, Preface, Introduction, or the Original TL;DR..............**7**

Before You Begin...**9**
#1: Ask Yourself — Do You *Really* Want to Program?.......................9
#2: (Good) Habits Save Time...9
#3: To B or Not To B...10

Know Your Basics...**11**
#4: Know the Lingo, Jack-O (or Jane-O)....................................11
#5: What's in a Name?...12
#6: Get That Functional Design Going......................................14
#7: Working Within Your Parameters..15
#8: Data — The Only Reason Anyone Really Programs.........................16
#9: Let's Talk Heaps About the Stack.......................................17
#10: Static and Scope and Global, Oh My!..................................18
#11: What the Hex Is Up With Binary and Octal?............................20
#12: That Is Most Logical, Mr. Boole......................................21
#13: Generic Algorithms — Let Them Be in Your Toolbox Forevermore.......22
#14: …Ditto for Data...23
#15: "OK," "Fine," "Fer Shur," and Other Regular Expressions..............24
#16: A Few Comments on Comments...25

Learn Your Craft, Earn Your Craft..**27**
#17: Connections Are Bad — Mostly...27
#18: Private First, Public If You Must....................................28
#19: Prefer Loose Couplings...29
#20: There's Always Exceptions to Exception Handling......................31
#21: Oopsie: Beware the Great Promise of "OOP"............................32
#22: Brand Everything...34
#23: Better, Faster, Stronger — The Basics................................34
#24: I Feel the Need, the Need for Speed (Unless This Phrase Is Trademarked, in Which Case I Just Have a Strong Preference for Going Faster)....................36
#25: Strings Only Pretend to Be Your Friend...............................37
#26: Threads, Twelve Step Programs, and Grey Hairs........................39
#27: Threading Your Way Through Threads Safely............................41
#28: Code Migration: Ready for Any "Port" in a Storm......................43
#29: IDE Should Stand for "I Don't Expect (To Program Without It)," or Something Like That..46
#30: A Workman's/Workwomen's/Workperson's Code Is Only as Sharp as His/Her/Their Tools...47

Discipline — The 20 in 80/20 51

#31: Don't Solve the Problem Too Soon 51
#32: Lose the Attitude, Find a New One, or Just Make It Better 52
#33: Just Code It Right, Right From the Start, Right? 54
#34: Code Like You May Need to Change Things, 'Cuz You Likely Will 55
#35: Inoculate Yourself Against NIH Syndrome 57
#36: Forget a To-Do List. Plan an "Oh-Oh" List 58
#37: Just Say "No" to Crap Code 59
#38: Know When to Break the Rules 61

Defensive Programming Is The Only Real Programming 63

#39: Ask Yourself: What If This Fails? 63
#40: Assume Nothing in Logic 65
#41: Floating Point Is a World Unto Itself 66
#42: The Simple Stuff'll Getyuh 68
#43: Cast Yea No More! 71
#44: Two (Computer) Minds Are Better Than One 72
#45: Don't Be a Hog 73
#46: Trust No One 74
#47: Invariably, Invariants Are Your Friend 75
#48: On Being Appropriately Testy 77

A GUI Is Worth 1,024 Words 81

#49: GUI Design is ALWAYS a Compromise 81
#50: Users Really Don't Care 82
#51: Annoyed User = Former User 83
#52: Understand the Battle Between Veterans and Newbies 85
#53: Remember Handicaps, Preconceptions 86
#54: Icons Are Stupid! 87
#55: Get Design Feedback 89
#56: A Little GUI (Change) Goes a Long Way 90
#57: Design With People In Mind — Specific People 91
#58: Pretty Is OK, But Beautiful Is Wonderful 92
#59: Help(ful) Files Have Their Place 93
#60: Moving Pictures Go Way Past Book Lernin' 95

Where Imagination Meets Reality: Debugging Your Code 97

#61: Understand the Problem of Testing 97
#62: Elementary, My Dear Debugger 98
#63: Tiptoe Thru the Digital Tulips 100
#64: Legacy Code Needs (Testing) Love Too 101
#65: Don't Hide Intermediates 103
#66: Leave No Bug Un-Understood 103
#67: A Repeatable Bug Is a Fixable Bug 104
#68: Document Bugs, No Matter How Embarrassing 105

After The Fun Is Done: Maintenance 107

#69: Lists? Check. Checklists? Double Check. Or, How to "Remember" to Do Everything
    Right the First Time 107
#70: Perfect Is the Enemy of Good Enough 108
#71: We Don't Need No Stinking Backups? 109
#72: Embrace Clean Running for the Next Time 111

Seeing The Big Picture: Project Requirements............113

#73: Battle Plans Never Survive the Battle...................................113
#74: Don't Prototype Yourself Into a Corner..................................114
#75: New Is the Enemy of Time...115
#76: Nothing Is as Constant as Change!...115
#77: Be Aware of Incomplete Requirements....................................117
#78: Measuring is Vital to Planning (and Finishing)........................118
#79: Keep Track of What Works For You...119

Dealing With People (Repeat After Me, A Programmer Is Not An Island)............121

#80: Code Is Clean, People Are Messy...121
#81: Be Nice..122
#82: Learn to Communicate Well...123
#83: Expect Part of Your Job to Be Educating.................................124
#84: Managements Woes...125
#85: You Manage People, Not Projects...126

The MBA Side Of Things: Programming As Your Business.....129

#86: Underpromise+Overdeliver..129
#87: Be Aware of (But Don't Follow) Sneaky Corporate Tricks............130
#88: Trust No Supplier...131
#89: Understand Where Customers Are REALLY Coming From...................132
#90: It's Your Business..133

Hacking Yourself............135

#91: You Change, We Change, They Change — Embracing the Inevitable....................135
#92: Ergonomics and You..136
#93: Learn to Manage Your Life..137
#94: Solve the Problem of How to Solve The Problem.......................138
#95: Embrace the Itch...139
#96: …And One Other Thing...140

Conclusion........143

About the Author........145

Forward, Preface, Introduction, or the Original TL;DR

This is the part you skip. So go ahead. Everyone does (I don't even know why people write forwards or prefaces or such).

Still here?

OK, this book is a short-but-sweet summary of what I think it takes to write quality code professionally, grouped into "rules" and "guidelines" or whatever else I feel like calling them. They've worked for me, and I've been programming for decades, so I should know something(?) If nothing else, the code I write works well, is maintainable, and keeps working, which is pretty much the whole purpose of being a programmer, isn't it?

Is that egotistical? Not really; much of this book is what I've gleaned from reading a whole lot of programming books, and then applying it, throwing out the awkward and silly stuff and refining the stuff that works. This book is your chance to avoid all the testing-then-rejecting of bad advice, and go with the advice that has helped me, and I truly hope will help you.

It's up to you to decide if everything in here is for you. Take what you want from it. Disagree with my views. Come up with better ones. But please, think about it. Reason on it. Because if programming is your job (and I think it's fair to say that, or you're going to get a surprise reading this book!) then you should be equipped for your job the best way you can.

I hope you get a lot out of the next pages, and that they give you some information to help become an even better programmer.

Let's get started…

Before You Begin...

Before we dive into Programming, The Craft, let's look at Programming, The Direction In Life...

#1: Ask Yourself — Do You *Really* Want to Program?

Do you like puzzles? Do you like solving problems? How about thinking analytically? Then you could be a good fit for programming.

Notice I didn't ask what the answers were. Not important. Frankly, there are too many people in the world that want to limit you. I personally believe that almost anyone can accomplish almost anything if they wish to bad enough (Notice the qualifiers? A good programmer watches out for absolutes!)

But seriously, programming can be a calling for some, just a well-paying job for another. It can be a lifelong career or a transitional pursuit. It's up to you.

However, if programming sounds good, for whatever reason, I can heartily recommend one thing — dedication and persistence (that's two things — oh, oh, I feel a Monty Python skit about the Spanish Inquisition starting up...)

But if you are going to program, strive to be a great one. As it says "Do you see any truly competent workers? They will serve kings rather than working for ordinary people." (Proverbs 22:29, New Living Translation Bible)

Work at being a great programmer, and you'll work for great people. And it doesn't hurt to start by reading and applying what's in the rest of this book...

#2: (Good) Habits Save Time

Can you remember every minute of your daily commute today? Or making the morning coffee? How about the shaving, showering, or makeup? If you've ever had a "how did I get here" moment, you are a victim (actually a beneficiary) of habits.

Simply put, habits occur when we do something long enough in the same way that the brain is comfortable going into "automatic drive." This is a very good thing as it lets the brain focus on more important matters.

OK, we are habit-making creatures — so what?

Because programming is full of examples where habits can save you time and mental energy.

Take for example naming variables. Do you spend endless seconds debating if "buff" is better, or to use "buf" instead? How about function names, simple code routines like `for` versus `while` loops, formatting, or even where you store your files on disk? In these cases, pick a standard way, stick to it, and let habits do the work for you in the future.

I'll be revisiting this point several times in this guide: Habits save effort. Any time you think about a solution you know you've done a dozen (or even a hundred) times before, make a choice, pick an option, note it somewhere, and then always do it that way. You'll soon find you're spending less time on the annoying minutiae and spending more time on the important stuff.

#3: To B or Not To B

(The caption makes marginally more sense if you know that the C language evolved from one called B.)

I don't want to start a religious war. I really don't. But if you look at a programming language index like TIOBE.com you'll see a little detail that few comment on: C and C++ are consistent popularity winners.

Combined, they account for more programmers than any other language. And yes, I know they are different dialects, but notice these indexes don't split Python up, even though v3.0 and v2.7 are incompatible; in contrast, most C compilers can also process C++.

Every month there's some comment or other about a new language shooting up the charts, but the fact is C & C++ is always up there.

But there's a more important reason you should be aware of C and C++: C is the granddaddy of a lot of languages.

Get familiar with the syntax of C and the class constructs of C++, and you'll find Java, Python, JavaScript, Objective-C, PHP, and many, many more languages easier to read and understand.

Of course, you likely have a favorite language already. But crack open a book or two on C/C++. Don't try to understand it all, but learn a little; it doesn't hurt to know something different. Like the mouse said after it scared off a cat by barking, "it's good to know a second language."

Know Your Basics

Why do armies have boot camp? Because there's a minimum basic training everyone needs before they move to the "big stuff" — so here's our boot camp of the basics for the well-rounded programmer...

#4: Know the Lingo, Jack-O (or Jane-O)

I once wrote a magazine article where I referred to the @ (at sign) character as the ampersand. Now in all fairness, the editor and proofreader missed it too, but the fact is I'm the technical author — so the proverbial buck stops here. And no one ever read an article and said "boy that proofreader sure doesn't know what he's talking about."

It's the same in programming. You make a mistake with a term and you look silly — the easier the term, the sillier you look. So get the basics down. At a minimum, learn fast the "code names" that you need in your neck of the woods (for example, if your programming language doesn't use "lambda functions" then less pressure to learn it). Don't forget spelling, and especially pronunciation — people really remember mispronounced words (I bet you can think right now of a few examples that you've heard).

Here's a list of symbols, mandatory for most every programming language, to get you started:

@ * & - Ampersand, oops, I mean at sign, followed by an asterisk and finally by the real ampersand.

` - Backtick, usually at the far left on a keyboard.

~ - The squiggly tilde (TILL-duh) often sharing the key with the backtick.

^ - Caret (kah-RAY)

\ and / - Back slash (or backslash) and forward slash — the "direction" is relative to right, presumably because we write from left to right and read the same way — so right is "forward" in the character.

{} [] () - Biggies to get right for programmers, they are the {braces}, [brackets], and (parenthesis) (that's pah-REN-tha-seeze for plural, pah-REN-tha-sis for singular).

| - Vertical bar (sometimes called a pipe).

- _ Dash or minus, along with underscore. Dashes get complicated if you do writing because they come in typographical formats as well, like em-dash (—) and en-dash (–). But minus or dash should be fine for code.

< > - Less than, greater than symbols. If in doubt, read from left to right, with the point on the smaller side. So 5 > 3 (greater than) and 3 < 5 (less than)

- Number sign. Also called the pound sign, but that can cause confusion with the British pound symbol.

And a bonus: Ordinal, cardinal, nominal. Think order, count, and name and you've got it. Example: Item 0 is a nominal (named) reference. It is the first (ordinal) item in a list of 12 (cardinal).

#5: What's in a Name?

"A rose by any other name would smell as sweet."

Garbage.

Call a rose a "poopy blossom" and see how easy it is to get $35 a dozen for them.

(Ok, "poopy blossom" was my first try for a name. You could do much better).

"Rose" is a word that conveys a mental image, a whole backstory that includes flowering plants, color, and aroma. And much more, including romance.

Words are shorthand for thoughts — and when you use rose instead of poopy blossom you give people a lot of information in a short word.

The point? Words matter. And as you name variables and functions in your code, you should understand this.

Call a variable "a" and it works just as well as "scrDX" — but when you're trying to figure out how wide the screen is, which variable looks like it will give you some help? I'll give you a hint — it's the one that begins "SCR" for screen and ends in "DX" for delta (change) in X. OK, maybe that's more than a hint.

Over time, your code will be awash in names: Function names, variable names, class names, and so on. It may seem faster to pick a quick name and move on — but a bit more time spent choosing a good name will save you a lot more time over the life of the code.

And when you get to code maintenance (and sooner or later someone will want you to tweak your old code) you will be glad you upgraded from "a" and "x" to something more recognizable.

So what to keep in mind when naming a variable?

• Know when to hold'em, and when to fold'em. The effort you spend naming a variable is directly proportional to its importance in the code. Loop variable? Call it `M` or `W` or something simple and move on. The status of the file I/O? Get it right, and name it `fileOpenStatus`.

• Be consistent. For far too long, I had used `buf` and `buff` interchangeably when writing code. It got to the point when I was alternating the spelling in a single function — and it wouldn't compile. So I took a moment, decided I liked `buff` more, and used that from then on. A little time and effort saved me tons of decision-making over the years (as I mentioned already regarding habits).

Likewise, don't use `DY` and `HEIGHT` both to describe height — pick one or the other. And if you frequently use `K` for a loop variable in functions, then why change it to `Z` in another?

• Stay with the group. Your organization might have a naming convention. Follow it. Even if it goes against the way you program, the benefit of everyone being on the same page outweighs it. You may have a hard day or two moving from `mousePressX` to `mouse_press_x`, but that's less effort overall than everyone else in the company having to learn to do it your way.

• Words are your friends. What exactly is `fobf`? No idea? But what if you renamed it `fileOutBuffer`? More letters, less ambiguity. Most modern development environments include refactoring/renaming variable names as a menu option, so no excuse not to make those names understandable at some point, or even renaming one entirely if a better name comes along.

• Case or underscore — pick one. I'm a fan of camelcase since it uses less characters and typing. Plus I like the look of `thisVariableName` over `this_variable_name`. You may differ. Again, just be consistent.

• Have a naming system to handle globals, locals, member variables, and so forth. Many conventions exist for how to describe a variable (for example, tacking an "i" to the front to indicate it's an integer). That's handy, but I prefer less about the type and more about the scope — is this a variable the whole world can see ("g" for global), or just the whole class ("m" for module); also, no prefix if visible only within a function. I find it's very important to know scope, to indicate who can tinker with a value. For example, how safe is it to change the use of `mScrDX` versus `gScrDX`? The former should only affect the code within the class, whereas the latter should warn you that a lot of code may break (not that you should have any global variables, but let's face it, it happens). And if it's just `scrDX` then the function is using it (but of course it may be a variable passed in by reference, and so technically not just local).

• Cautiously add type info to a name. Compilers catch a lot of errors, so I don't have to worry I'll accidentally place the pointer for a string into an integer variable. On the other hand, for things some compilers might miss (like signed/unsigned copying, or code that has lots of casting) you may wish to add type info, like "u" in front if unsigned, or "ps" for a pointer to a string.

• Do add value info, especially when it's nonstandard. A lot of errors occur when people assume units not obvious (look at the number of space probes lost over the years from silly conversion mistakes). So is the value in seconds or milliseconds? Then it's `timeSec` or `timeMS`. This is not contrary to the previous point — the compiler and IDE can still tell me if it's a short or a long or a float — but the value is understood by me to be something specific. Plan to change "timeSec" to "timeDay" and I know the code needs rewriting — which is key to a good variable name.

• Don't confuse people. I once wrote a PHP obfuscator that changed all variables to variations of v and w — `$wwwv`, `$wvww`, `$wwvwwv`, etc. The purpose was to make it hard to tell variables apart, and therefore harder to decode the program. However, we usually want to make code more readable, so unless confusion is your goal, avoid variables with I and 1 close together, O and 0, etc. I even avoid using j in loops because i and j look similar. Same with m and n, so I tend to nest loops `i`; `k`; `m` — but that's my Fortran background, where those variables were considered integers, ideal for fast loops.

#6: Get That Functional Design Going

Like variables, a good function name can help a program, and a bad one, well, you know.

But functions are a little different: Variables are the nouns of the programming world, whereas functions are the verbs. Functions do things to variables, so they need different naming conventions — here's some tips:

• Be aware of object/action versus action/object when naming. If you flash a memory chip in a function, do you call it `FlashMemory()` or `MemoryFlash()`? Your choice, but be consistent. I prefer placing the object first, since then I can group the functions alphabetically yet logically: `MemoryCheck()`, `MemoryFlash()`, `MemoryRepair()` and so on all affect the memory, whereas `FlashMemory()`, `FlashDrive()`, and `FlashRAM()` don't really feel like they belong together — same operation but different objects. This also aligns with object-oriented programming, where the variable comes before the function, enforcing object/action: `mMemory.Check()`, `mMemory.Flash()`, `mMemory.Repair()`, etc.

• Make function calls focused and clear. Sending out a print job? Then `Print-erJobStart()` makes more sense than `PrinterInit()` (what are we "init"ing — the printer, or a single job?) Be specific, and don't be afraid to rename functions if they change meaning as you code or update them.

• Try to always be positive. If your function returns a boolean or flag, never use a negative — our brains hate parsing double negatives, and they don't enjoy single negatives much either. After all, which is quicker/easier to figure out:

```
if (PrinterIsBusy())
if (not PrinterisNotBusy())
```

• Try to avoid entirely multipurpose functions. I personally have a real weakness with these — take a function, and with a small tweak, make it multipurpose. For example, if a parameter is 1, return a value; if 2, process it, etc. `realloc()` in C is an example of this: If you pass it NULL, it gives you a new memory chunk, but if you give it a memory pointer, it'll resize it instead. In theory it sounds good, since you're avoiding code duplication, and it keeps the logic all in one place. However, now the function is a grab-bag of code for slightly different uses. Rule of thumb: If you have a hard time giving the function one clear and descriptive name, you're likely trying to do too many things at once. In my experience, once you go the "flag" route, the function will come back and haunt you as you try to maintain the code, and it gets more and more "slightly different" each time you edit it. Instead, split the function into several, and even form them into a class if possible.

#7: Working Within Your Parameters

So you've got your function name — now time to add parameters:

• Name parameters well. The same rules apply here as they do for variables, since of course that's what they are.

• Consistent parameter lists for common functions. In the Windows API, messages contain a handle value (hWnd) and two parameters, a long value and double long/wide (lParam and wParam). Windows functions that use this data tend to include all three even if they don't need them; by passing all three, and always in the same order, the programmer can write the calls easily, rather than checking if (for example) a specific function requires lParam after wParam, or just wParam.

• Parameters and flexibility. Sometimes a function becomes more robust if you move code or values into a user-provided parameter. For example, `qsort()` is a function that requires another function passed to it as a parameter — this second function tells `qsort()` how to compare your specific data. The extra function makes it general purpose; without it, it could only sort one kind of data.

• Testing. I find often the parameters come up naturally when I think of testing the function. For example, a global called from within the function is hard to test — but pass that same global variable as a function parameter, and you can test easier.

• Watch out for constant versus references values. Many modern languages allow you to pass parameters in one of two ways: Constant, where changing the parameter's value in the function doesn't affect the original value outside of the function, and changeable, where it does. Try for constant as much as possible. If you make a parameter changeable, the user of the function has to keep a mental note in their head that the outside variable might be affected, which can get confusing. For example, I often see questions online as to why this function or that doesn't work right with strings. Usually it's a case of the function changing the original string when it wasn't expected, or not changing it when it was. Side effects like that should be watched carefully, and it might even be worthwhile to change the function name to be clearer: For example, `AppendToCopy()` versus `AppendToString()`.

• Return only what you need. For years, I always added a return value to my functions — and then rarely used them. Over time, I realized I was having maintenance issues because I had never needed or tested the return value, and sometimes it didn't work right when I eventually tried to use it. Better no return value until you need it than a time bomb when you do.

#8: Data — The Only Reason Anyone Really Programs

No matter what language you use, you'll be digging into data in no time. So knowing the types of data you'll work with are vital.

Many books draw a line between intrinsic data types, such as integer and float and string, versus classes or structures and so forth. I prefer to think in terms of memory usage — items that can be passed all at once (integer, boolean, long, pointer, etc) and those that are too big to pass easily, and need to be passed by reference (pointers). This division includes arrays, classes, structures, floating point variables, and the ubiquitous string (for the purists, I know it is possible to pass large objects directly, but many languages make this hard to do, and there is often a performance hit, so I'll skip it here).

Thinking about data this way is valuable. You automatically think in terms of performance when writing code. Otherwise, using a class or structure seems as simple as using an integer, and floating point and integer seem identical. For example, look at this Visual BASIC code:

```
Dim X as string="1"
Dim Y as integer=1
```

Looks almost the same, doesn't it? But behind the scenes Y sets up a space for an integer, and then puts 1 in it. X however sets up space for a pointer to the string, then looks for available memory space to hold the string, then reserves that space, then moves the character "1" into it, and finally sets that string space pointer value into X. Finding space for a string is time consuming, and a whole lot more is happening in that string assignment compared to the integer assignment.

Now of course, if you need a string, use a string. Just be aware that the time difference in using a string is much larger than using an integer. Languages that blend the two (PHP comes to mind) do the newer programmer a disservice by making it seem that everything is simple and cheap to do, whereas nothing could be further from the truth (and by the way, yet another reason to learn C, since using pointers teaches you quickly which items are "tiny" performance-wise and which ones aren't).

Besides the difference in data size, how they are stored can also byte you (!) on the tuchus. For example, I've been hit by this issue many times:

```
unsigned short X=1;
...later on...
X=-1;
...still later on...
if (X<0) // never happens!
```

Today's compilers will catch this and warn you, but the result is that -1 to you is actually 65535 to X, because it doesn't understand signs or negative numbers, and -1 and 65535 are the same internally in the variable.

Notice also the "short" — if I had used "int" the unsigned value for -1 would vary, since in C the int is considered the ideal size for the computer it's running on — which could be a 64-bit Windows machine, or a 16-bit micro-controller. In contrast, short is usually a 16 bit value; and if I wanted to be precise, I could use the definition uint16_t which should be available on most compilers.

#9: Let's Talk Heaps About the Stack

Languages like C get you peeking under the hood. You learn about performance because everything is so low level. Want a string? Learn to use malloc() and free() or otherwise manage memory yourself (or move to C++ and use its String class).

Now that's great when you need to code "close to the metal," but most times you just want a program to work, simply and easily. Ideally you'd have the best of both worlds, and you can: Understand where performances issues generally pop up, and you can program without constant fussing on low-level details (usually).

Take the stack. In the previous tip I explained all the effort that goes into getting a string set up. For example, `malloc()` has to wander through a list of memory chunks looking for an open spot (sort of like a waiter finding a table for a party of ten in a crowded restaurant). That lookup can take a long time, and is typical when you store things on the heap, the general memory of the computer. But if you use the stack, here's the equivalent in C:

```
char buff[]="My string";
```

The stack pointer tells the computer where you are in the program: When a function is called, the current location is added to the stack (called pushing) and then the function is run. When it ends, the address on the stack is grabbed (called popping) and the program goes back there. But that stack also can hold data. In our example, to make a local copy of this string, the stack pointer is adjusted to skip over a section, the string is copied into that section, and you're good. No searching for a memory chunk.

The takeaway? The stack is VERY FAST.

The stack is faster than the heap, but at a cost. Often, there's much less stack space to work with. Also, if you write beyond the data's "edge" you damage more than data, since the stack is used for program control (of course, damaging the heap isn't a lot better, but your program code is unaffected, so it might survive a little longer!)

Plus, the stack is transitory. Create something there and when you leave the function, the variable disappears (kinda; the data is still there but good programming dictates you never try to access it again, so we'll all just pretend it disappears).

So small, fast but temporary, versus large, slow and semi-permanent. That is the great conflict in software. Picking which is key to fast functions and a fast program. For example, using a `char[]` buffer versus the C++ `String` class will give you a huge difference in speed, if you can fit the string on the stack without issues.

And then sometimes you can have a compromise, like a static variable — but along with that comes issues of scope…

#10: Static and Scope and Global, Oh My!

Static is a handy crossbreed — a variable you can create fast like a local stack variable, but it stays around like a heap variable. Sounds good, but with the benefits comes issues.

If I have a variable on the stack, it has local scope — outside of that function, no one knows anything about it, and when the function ends, it evaporates in a puff of digital smoke.

However, a static variable stays forever, from the start of the program till the very end. And it can be the exact opposite of a local variable, with global scope, visible to all (although it doesn't have to be).

You might think that's a great compromise. But memory for the static is kept around a long time, which is a problem if you need a lot of statics, or some big ones. And this is special memory, since the static starts as part of the program, embedded in the executable program's file. Every megabyte of data there expands the program by a megabyte as well. And quite likely, that megabyte requires another megabyte of working memory (heap) to store the statics when the program runs!

Scope is also an issue; global scope means every function in the program can monkey with it, and over time this monkeying gets messier and messier. You'll lose track of where that variable was changed, and by whom. And little changes get big fast when that variable affects a hundred different functions. And so on. This is the reason why you avoid globals as much as possible.

Of course not all static variables are global in scope. For example, a class can have a static variable that is private in scope, so only visible to code within the class. For example, say you want every object to have a unique id. Create a static counter, then increment and pass the value every time an object needs it. Here's some C++ code:

```
class myLittleClassy
{
  private:
    static long sPoolID=0;
    long mUniqueID;
  public:
    myLittleClassy()
    {
      // every object gets a unique id!
      mUniqueID=++sPoolID;
    }
};
```

So global statics are bad, but private statics are fine, right? Not always. Without getting into too much detail, testing functions becomes an issue when statics are involved, since you now have to include them and their values/side effects. The result is more complicated testing code. Over time I've learned to minimize statics as much as possible because of these issues (although I'm still partial to using them for unique ids!) Private statics are better than global ones, but they still can be a burden, so use them cautiously.

#11: What the Hex Is Up With Binary and Octal?

If you know 0xFF is 255 and 0xFFFF is -1 (or 65,535) you can probably skip this one.

If you don't, you are missing out on learning the computer's native language. And you'll find it a lot harder to communicate in programming if you don't speak CPU.

A bit is an on/off signal (technically, different voltage levels in circuits). In the old days (I'm talking magnetic core memory days — look it up), binary valued bits were grouped into triplets, with two-to-the-power-of-three or 8 possible states, called octal. In octal, the next number after 7 is not 8, but 10, and so 20 octal is 16 decimal, and 100 octal is 64 decimal (eight times eight, just as 100 decimal is ten times ten).

Today, octal is the Rubik's cube of the computer world: Fun to show off, but completely useless from a practical standpoint (I should know, since I learned how to solve a Rubik's cube when I was young).

Now binary can also be grouped into quartets rather than triplets, and that's where hex comes in. Hexadecimal handles two-to-the-power-of-four (normally written as 2^4) or 16 values. Early processors like the Intel 8008 got us used to data sizes of 4 and 8 bits, so hex was a great fit, a more compact way to handle individual bits.

You'll encounter these sixteen values often in programming, since they are the pathway to communicating with the computer's lower levels. So at a minimum you should learn hex, and ideally a "bit" of binary (sorry!) Memorize the places from 10 to 15 (A-F) and get a feel for how combining hex digits gives you bigger numbers (it's all powers of 16, so for example 1A is 1*16+10*1, or 26).

Though hex is compact and handy, individual bits are beneficial too. For example, you'll encounter them if you do masking. Here, the question of "even or odd" is answered simply with binary in C:

```
if ( a & 1 )
```

In most processors, the AND (&) operator converts to a very fast operation, and the single 1 means only the last binary digit of the number is kept (the rest of the number is zero, and as "0 & Anything" is always zero, the rest of the result stays zero). This means that the command "masks out" or hides the other bits, only showing the last digit, and whether it is 1 or 0, or odd/even, and usually much quicker than the modulo operator a % 1.

#12: That Is Most Logical, Mr. Boole

Spock had it easy; logic is usually quite alien for the rest of us. And a special type of logic is even harder, called Boolean logic (named after, quite logically, a Mr. George Boole). For this logic, we have to limit ourselves to yes/no answers. The benefit? It's the way computers "think," and with this knowledge we become CPU whisperers.

So at a minimum, you'll need to understand the types of operators, their precedence, and the logical versus bitwise versions, and even some specific to your language (for example the "===" and "!==" operators in PHP for exact matches of contents and type).

The previous tip showed the C/C++ & operator in action, which was bitwise. The "&&" in contrast is logical, and uses the whole value for comparisons, making it more human-like (for instance we tend to consider 0 as false, and 125 as true, rather than what their individual bits might represent). Whereas `a & 1` told us if the last bit of a number was on/off, `a && 1` tells us if the whole number is off (zero) or on (any other number but zero); and likewise `a && b` would tell us if both variables were nonzero (true) or either were zero, or both were zero (false).

Precedence is important to know, since without parenthesis to help, those are the rules that give the exact result — for example, we know that multiply is handled before addition if there are no parenthesis, and so it is with logical operators (but there's never any harm in adding parenthesis and skipping the guessing game for other programmers reading your code!) In computer languages, "!" (NOT, or negation) is processed first, followed by "&&" (AND), then "||" (OR) — of course, what they are called varies; but since many languages have C roots, it should be close.

That's the minimum for creating statements; for manipulating them, I recommend a little more. A huge part of programming for me is reversing `if()` statements, combining or breaking them up, or otherwise rearranging them. For example, say you want to reverse `a==0` — it's pretty easy, `a!=0`. But what about `a>0`? The answer is not `a<0` but `a<=0` remembering to include the equals sign. (Unclear why? Play computer and imagine `a=0` — in the first test it fails, but it succeeds in the last one, which is what reversing should do.)

That's a single term, but how about reversing this?

```
if ( price>10 && style!=2 && style!=4 )
```

Ouch. But here's a standby from logic that has helped me rearrange `if()` statements without making a mistake — all courtesy of another Mister, Mr. De Morgan:

```
NOT ( A OR B) = ( NOT A ) AND ( NOT B )
NOT ( A AND B) = ( NOT A ) OR ( NOT B )
```

Notice the pattern? When we move the negation (NOT) to apply to individual elements, we reverse the "inter-element" symbols AND for OR and vice versa. With De Morgan's laws it's much easier to manipulate logic statements.

Take our example; of course, one easy way to reverse it is to surround the whole thing with parenthesis and then negate it all:

```
if ( ! ( price>10 && style!=2 && style!=4 ) )
```

Now, for complicated logic statements this can be handy and somewhat easier to understand. But let's say you plan to break this into multiple `if()` statements later on. So to negate it the De Morgan way, we surround each test with parenthesis and then negate those parts, also negating the logical operators in between; so reversing

```
if ( (price>10) && (style!=2) && (style!=4) )
```

becomes

```
if ( !(price>10) || !(style!=2) || !(style!=4) )
```

We reverse each statement, eliminating the "!" here to get the simpler opposite:

```
if ( (price<=10) || (style==2) || (style==4) )
```

(Notice again the reverse of `price>10` is `price<=10` not `price<10`).

Throw some numbers at it and see that it works. De Morgan to the rescue!

#13: Generic Algorithms — Let Them Be in Your Toolbox Forevermore

Do you know your quicksort from your bubble sort? Your sequential search from your binary search? Are all random number generators created equal? How about Huffman versus RLE (run line encoding) compression?

Your coding will be dominated by algorithms, the steps to getting things done in the computer world. Some, like searching and sorting, are used everywhere; others, like compression or random numbers, are more specialized but still commonly used.

When I was a wee slip of a programmer, bubble sort and linear search worked fine. Easy to write, and write "right" (nothing tricky, like coding a binary search). But as I (and my data) grew, I moved to more advanced algorithms that gave better performance. After all, a linear search on 30 items will take about 15 checks on average, and about 5 with a binary search — not a big difference. But by the time you get to 999,999 items you'll need about 499,999 sequential comparisons on average, whereas a binary search needs only 20 or so.

Even now, I still occasionally use bubble sort — but I know exactly when and where to use it. For example, if a list will never get bigger than five items, bubble sort can be coded in place and give fine performance. That's the confidence that comes from knowing various sorting algorithms, and picking the one that does "good enough."

At a minimum, sit down with a book or two on basic algorithms. Go to Wikipedia and work through the "List of algorithms." Start with understanding what they do; then try to understand why you'd pick one over the other, and when. Finally, get to know the nooks and crannies, and especially any problems you may encounter.

I once had an example of how "nooks and crannies" knowledge can help in debugging. A display grid had horrible refresh speeds after a column sort, even though the sort routine was quicksort, which normally has excellent performance. "Normally" is the key of course: A little-mentioned fact is that when all the data is identical or nearly identical, quicksort no longer quickly sorts. You can code a workaround to minimize the problem (as most versions do), but this code was by the grid's author and didn't include the workaround. Ergo, really slow sorts when the data was similar.

The fix involved changing the sort fields to include the line number. This guaranteed each entry would be unique, and so also guaranteed sorting would perform at maximum speed. Problem solved, because I knew about this exception in the quicksort algorithm.

Abraham Lincoln is presumed to have said "Give me six hours to chop down a tree and I will spend the first four sharpening the axe." Sharp tools make easy work. In programming, algorithms do the work, but if we don't know how to use them, they might as well not be there. So perhaps the programming quote could be "Keep sharp about algorithms, and you won't be a tool six hours from now." Or something like that.

#14: ...Ditto for Data

Marshall McLuhan is famous for saying "The medium is the message," pointing out that the channel used to convey information influences the message (for example, the message presented by a TV News report versus the web page version, or movies versus their book versions).

For computer programming, the phrase could perhaps be changed to "The data is the algorithm." How we view data is intertwined with what we want to do with it. We use dictionary objects when we want quick access via a key; in contrast, we'd use a list when locating by indexed position or via random access matters more.

What we want to do with data can shape early on how we organize and store it. Say you're reading in numbers and need to keep them in sorted order. If speed of input is vital and you only need the final results, then a fast array (which can add an item to the list's end easily) and a single final sort should do the trick; if it's more important to have the list constantly ordered as data is read in, then a sorted dictionary trades more individual item updating for always having the data sorted. Same data, but the needs of the program dictate how it's maintained.

So picking the best data component is well worth a bit of studying. Grab books on the data groups/objects your language supports and study what each is best for. And if you want more on the give and take of data versus algorithms, I recommend "Programming Pearls" by Jon Bentley.

#15: "OK," "Fine," "Fer Shur," and Other Regular Expressions

In this book I try to be language agnostic — after all, programming is programming — so why recommend a specific language, regular expressions?

Because regular expressions is a tool available to almost every language. So instead of a language, think of it as a vocabulary you add to any language for a specific purpose. Take for example using my text editor to clean text. If I have it search and replace this:

```
^\s*(.*)\s*$
```

with this

```
$1
```

It removes leading and trailing spaces from each line. The ^ and $ denote the start and end of the line, respectively; the \s refers to a space character (actually all whitespace, so it includes tabs and other "invisible" characters), while the period refers to any character. And the asterisk? It refers to quantity, where \s* means zero or more whitespace characters. Taken together, the message is "take a whole line, and grab all the spaces at the start, then other characters, and all the spaces at the end." Only the matched text (the .* within the parenthesis) is kept, and it's placed back into the text using $1. Result? Leading and trailing spaces go buh-bye.

This just scratches the surface, but it shows you how regular expressions are used. I find them invaluable when I need to massage data. For instance, if I'm given a list of items in the wrong order, I can reverse them with a similar search and replace. Say the two items are separated by a comma. Then search on

```
^([^,]+),([^,]+)$
```

and replace with

```
$2,$1
```

Same line start/end character codes, but now two groups in parenthesis, which we swap in the results (second group ahead of first). The text in the brackets is used to include a character list — in this case, the comma, and the caret ("^") is used to negate. Combined with a new counting character (+, which refers to one or more characters, unlike * which means zero or more characters) and we get "go through a line from start to finish, collecting all non-comma characters in group $1, then skip the comma, and then group all the non-comma characters into a second group $2." Finally, place them in the result text in opposite order, adding a comma in between.

As you can see, regular expressions make easy work of text manipulation. Besides using them in an editor to do text massaging like reversing list items, they are also useful in code. Typically they fall into the following groups:

• Searching/Matching. This function is usually called something like match or grep, after the UNIX command. You often need to find text, but sometimes a straight search is not generic enough. Need to find all 2 digit numbers? Then you need a grep-style search, and a filter like [^\d]\d\d[^\d] (find one non-digit with [^\d] then two digits with \d and then another non-digit).

• Splitting. Sometimes it's easier to search on the differences; getting rid of them, and keeping everything that doesn't match. For example, if all the data is separated by commas, splitting on \s*,\s* will give you a cleaned list (no leading/trailing spaces as well, thanks to each \s*), and works with every other character (except embedded commas of course).

• Replacing. Finding the text usually returns matches. Occasionally, you want to manipulate the matches and put them back into the text, like capitalizing the first letter of every word. This type of function lets you specify the replacement data, or optionally call a function with the matches, so you can modify them and return the changes to be inserted automatically. One search I've used a lot in writing this book is \s\s+ (search on 2 or more whitespace characters in a row) and replace with a single space, getting rid of accidentally doubled or tripled (or more) spaces.

No matter what language you use, explore how they support regular expressions and try them out. You'll likely find it a lot easier than "rolling your own" code for many kinds of text massaging, searching, and filtering jobs.

#16: A Few Comments on Comments

"A word fitly spoken is like apples of gold in pictures of silver," says Proverbs 25:11.

Three thousand years ago, a carved golden apple embedded in a picture made of silver must have been quite impressive to look at, hence the Bible's comparison to speaking well. Comments are today's version of "golden apples" in programming — the right word can make all the difference. How then should we best use our words?

• Fundamentally, a comment should add to the code. If the code isn't obvious, then the comment has a clear job — to clarify. Don't get me wrong, code should be clear and easy to understand, and therefore comments explaining it few and far between. But in the real world, complicated code does get shipped. If you have trouble understanding what you did in a function, and how, that's a warning flag to you that the function may not be in the best shape. At least document it!

• Comment for newbies. In many shops, the veteran programmers do new code, and the newbies do maintenance. Help them make sense of it with a few notes. Watch jargon, references to obscure algorithms (at least without some help in researching them) and so on. I make a point of including informational URLs when needed, but also explaining what the URL should contain, just in case the Internet disappears (or at least that URL). After all, if you don't make a comment newbie-friendly, their only reasonable option is to ask you directly, harshing your mellow and breaking your flow. So you're really doing yourself a favor, not them, right?

• Comments are for you too. Simple test: I find if I have trouble explaining the code the very next day, then it needs further documentation. This also has a great side effect of getting you into the code again, possibly catching subtle errors you missed the first time around. In fact, a good rule of thumb is that if the code is hard to explain now, it will cause you further problems down the line. Explaining in the comments goes a long way to testing yourself if you've really figured it out.

• Comment the unexpected. Did the code act oddly in testing? Is this algorithm tweaked in a weird (unexpected) way? Whatever the reader/programmer needs to get up to speed, put it in, and help them get up to speed — and save time.

• Comment hard-won knowledge. Somebody didn't read this book, and six months later, you are digging through their code wishing there were more comments. Once you have the answer, do you then add your knowledge via comments? If you don't want to dig through the code again six more months down the line, the answer is obvious. And what to document is also obvious — what you just learned. You (or someone else) will thank you someday.

• Comments need to be maintained. Guaranteed, you will forget the details of that change you just made. Quickly patched the function but didn't update the comment about the fix? Then you'll be unhappy down the line when you've forgotten the tweak and digging through the code doesn't explain why such-and-such happens. I'm a staunch believer that programmers should maintain their own code for a year or two after writing it so they experience firsthand code without enough comments, or out of sync comments — and no one to blame but themselves!

The fact is, any odd or unusual method is a pain to look into as time passes. If you maintain code (something I recommend for any programmer, senior or junior) you'll soon learn that no matter what you write, time can rearrange the lines of code into a cold sticky porridgey mess no one wants to stir up, let alone dig into. So help everyone out — comment.

Learn Your Craft, Earn Your Craft

I firmly believe the difference between a good programmer and a great programmer is how they care about the work. Viewing it as a job versus viewing it as a craft makes a real difference. Perception is everything, not just to others, but internally to yourself. Craftsmen (Craftswomen? Craftspersons?) care about doing it right, as opposed to just doing it. Here then is a list of tips that all crafts-beings should appreciate.

#17: Connections Are Bad — Mostly

When I wrote the word "Mostly" I heard in my head that little kid in Aliens. You know, the one that said about the monsters there that they "come out at night — mostly." It's that little add-on of "mostly" that says daytime is not as safe as you'd expect, and sometimes you might end up just a little bit dead.

Same with connections in code. Data has to interact, so we need connections. But connections grow fast and can bite back painfully if you're not careful.

You may know the formula about connections, known as Metcalfe's Law:

`n = c(c-1)/2`

So if two classes (c) connect there's only one link (n) between them. Three classes, three connections. But then it grows fast; by 10 classes there can be 45 connections!

That's simplified. Classes or forms or functions or an individual programmer's code section often share many more items. A global variable may be shared across dozens of classes or files, and so each change has to be monitored to make sure it doesn't break somewhere else. As the program grows, this becomes very, very tough.

Keeping that many items in mind at the same time is a challenge. Some people enjoy it — some don't. But I guarantee that after an extra-fun weekend of [insert favorite activity here] you won't be in the mood (or shape) to come back to work and juggle as many things as you usually do.

So plan for that. At a minimum, watch out for global data. Encapsulate it in a class or structure if at all possible, so you can track it better. Even a structure of a dozen global settings is still better that a dozen individual globals scattered throughout code.

Continuing this, wrap external globals or values you can't manage yourself. Need the screen width? Make a function to return the value and have your code always call that. Now, you've reduced the many connections to the operating system's screen width down to one. This avoids different programmers creating different calls with different parameters, and so reduces upgrading issues in the future.

For example, if one programmer calls for the screen width of the main screen, and another does a call for the current screen, then computers with multiple monitors have a bug waiting to happen when the user works on the secondary monitor. Place the call in one function and that one fix keeps everyone on the same (screen) page.

Always keep a sharp eye out for connections and prune them aggressively.

#18: Private First, Public If You Must

Metcalfe's Law is scary as things get big, but that's part of the problem: It starts small and easy to manage, since not all those connections spring up at once.

Maybe you program the first five connections or so, classes that need to share data. You aren't too worried about access, so some of it starts out global for easier/faster coding.

Then management says how about a new feature, and that feature needs more details from the rest of your code. So you add code to use those classes. More connections. Then another change. Then another. And so on. Before you know it, that globally-accessible data is used all over the place, and each of those connections has to be monitored.

The solution? Make everything private by default, and only allow public access after some strenuous evaluation.

Now I'm not talking about locking down small general-purpose classes, like something for complex numbers or a rectangle. But a larger, more detailed class or object needs more careful planning.

Take for example a business database where everyone can read and write its data variables directly. But one programmer forgets that money values are written in integer pennies instead of fractional decimal dollars (thereby avoiding fractions and round-off). One programmer writes the date and time in UTC and another writes it in local time. And so on.

Clearly, these many connections directly to the database need pruning. So the first step is to circulate rules, which everyone promptly forgets or ignores. Next step is to create an API for the database, and everyone has to go through it. A function like `DBWritePriceInPennies()`, while looking blocky and odd, reminds everyone how to store money values. Grudgingly, people use the new API (except when they don't) and the database is protected.

Eventually, you close off the DB's direct access by hiding connection and access details from everyone, and now even the stragglers are forced to use the API; and then — finally — the database is consistent.

So you've solved some of the connection issues by funneling access to a few routines. But if you'd started with protected data, and access through a minimal set of routines, you could have avoided the extra work in the first place.

Now you may be thinking that preventing errors with integer pennies versus floating point dollars is one thing — what about the times? A UTC time looks like local time, just shifted for the timezone (unless your database is in Greenwich England of course), so what stops someone from slipping up and the compiler allowing it? But here again keeping things private first helps. For instance, what if all times are transaction times, so they're the current time when the function is called? Then no programmer needs to directly fiddle with times — the calling function adds the timestamp when a record is created or updated, transparently and accurately.

What if some dates need to be editable? Then a pair of functions `LocalToUTC()` and `UTCToLocal()` could augment the database routines, which, like the dollar amounts, could reference the data style: `SetUpdateUTC()` or `SetUpdateLocalTime()`. Combined, you can access the field, but still be reasonably certain the date won't be messed with. And as a bonus, because you publish the calling routines at the start, there's less chance a programmer will roll their own (possibly error-prone) routine, since the necessary ones already exist.

Looking at these examples, it's obvious that locking down access early saves time later — time in coding, debugging mistakes in coding, and then fixing things when assumptions go wrong. So be stingy about data access as long as possible.

#19: Prefer Loose Couplings

OK, your data is private, and you're stingy about connections. But you still need to share some data. How best then? Prefer loose coupling.

Coupling is related to how interdependent the parts and connections are. In programming, tight coupling is just like a tight joint in the real world: Hard to pry apart when you need to, and likely requiring a custom fitting when you do replace or repair it.

To prevent that, you can write routines that reduce coupling whenever possible, and also avoid relying on the details of other functions/objects/data as much as possible:

• Don't use any internals of a function's return value not explicitly stated. Say a function returns an internal value, doubling as a flag. For example, `strcmp()` can return the difference between two characters, with the sign of that difference determining whether it is less than, greater than, or equal to zero (which string if "higher" or "lower"). According to the specification, only the sign should be relied on, not the difference value. However, what if in some exotic code you use that value directly? When you do that, the coupling becomes very tight. The code is now tough to change without breaking (also called brittle). As well, a problem arises if someday a new version of `strcmp()` only returns -1, 0 and +1.

• Returning/filtering the minimum data. People will use internal values even if they shouldn't. For that reason I'll often clean up values I want to return as boolean, forcing them to true or false with a call like

```
return ( 0==x ? false : true );
```

Imagine a routine that returns the balance from an account, but all you want is if they are above or below a limit (for example, over-drafted or not). Return a boolean only, say in a function like `IsOverdraft()` and you don't have to worry about people using function return values to also get bank account balances — a potentially huge security issue!

• Prevent access to raw data for all but the simplest of classes. Many languages make it easy to implement setter/getter functions for variables, and at a minimum you should use that. If a value can be read or written directly from outside a class, you risk code getting too dependent on specifics, and tighter coupling. Think of a home: If people knock on the door and you meet them there, they have no idea how it's decorated, what pictures are on the wall, etc. But let anyone knocking come in and sit in your favorite chair, and they get expectations. Maybe they want a certain channel on TV, with their dinner following right after!

Inviting other code into a class is like that. Say you have a complex number class, with two decimal values, one for real and one for imaginary parts. But you need a lot of them, and have a brainstorm how you can pack them into less memory and save space. If other code can reach in, they all have to be taught this new method of packing/unpacking your complex numbers. But if you have setter/getter functions, nothing outside the class changes. In large and complex programs, meeting them at the doorway can mean a lot less work.

• Avoid coding schizophrenic return values. It's sometimes tempting to pack more into the return, but be careful. I once coded a "near" binary search, which returned the nearest match index (the item less than or equal the value) and also a flag indicating whether it was a match or not (this function found the data match, or failing that, told me the index of the highest item item less than the match). And I tried to pack it into a single integer return value.

Learn Your Craft, Earn Your Craft

Bad idea. I'd use a positive value for true, negative for false, so -5 meant item #5 was just a near match. But of course item #0 has no sign, so to avoid returning it I'd added +1 to the index before I included the sign flag; now -6 would mean item #5 was a near match. But there's more: if nothing was matching or lower I'd need to return -1, which meant I needed to add +2 to each index so that I never returned 0. Complicated enough? Imagine documenting it! In the end, +7 would mean a match for item #5. Now THAT is tight coupling, because every calling function would have to know A) how to extract the flag sign value, B) make the value positive, and C) then take away 2 to get the index! Fortunately, I caught myself before finishing this mess, and went back to returning the found/not found flag and the index separately.

In plumbing a loose coupling can flood a basement; but in programming, a loose coupling saves the day.

#20: There's Always Exceptions to Exception Handling

Exception handling is a fantastic way to writing cleaner code — when it's done right. When not, it's painful:

• Exception handling, is, well, for exceptional events. I once used exception code to clean up a data object — if the object's date was invalid, throw an exception, if the ID was invalid, throw an exception, and so on. The exception handler then massaged the data into shape, or passed back an error. The result was (usually) a validated object.

I was quite tickled by the code, until I added a new field to the object, which meant upgrading all the old objects to include the new valid field. To handle that, I just placed more code in the exception handler; when old objects failed (because of missing the field) I exceptioned out and generated the new field's data.

And the code stalled.

It took quite a bit of research to find the culprit, but in the end it turned out that code with exception handling is very fast when there is no problem, but painfully slow if activated. By making every old object throw an exception, I was bogging down the system in extra error handling, and believe me, it was some serious bogging.

I rewrote the code to handle the upgrade silently without throwing, and a valuable lesson was learned: Use exception handling everywhere, but don't USE exception handling ANYWHERE! (I thought this was pithier than "always code exception handling, but don't use exception throwing as part of regular program flow.")

• Another dusty corner of exception handling is that not all is throwable. In theory you should be able to catch every exception somehow. For example, C++ has "`catch (...)`" that will do this in one statement. But in reality, there are always exceptions to this rule (let's call them "exception exceptions.")

For example, in .NET code there is a managed (C#/VB) part and potentially an unmanaged part (C/C++ code, DLL, operating system, etc). I've actually tracked down a bug where the unmanaged code has exceptions that can't be caught. So keep that in mind when bulletproofing code — there is a limit.

• Likewise, not all is exceptional. Adding too much exception code, while not a performance penalty (unless thrown, remember) is extra code that can slow down our understanding of a function. Much like a bygone era's GOTO, we humans have to follow all the jumps "just in case" — necessary if the code is important, but a lot of mental gymnastics for code that doesn't need it. So if you add two numbers, you likely don't need a try/catch in case of an overflow exception — unless you expect someone to deliberately add two very large numbers.

Exception handling is a sweet way to code — but remember, we all need to pay attention to our sweets.

#21: Oopsie: Beware the Great Promise of "OOP"

OOP (Object-Oriented Programming) is encapsulation.

There — I said it. Classes are great and interesting and useful, but fundamentally they are encapsulation, a walled garden between the world and the object's data.

As you might gather by now, I'm a fan of object encapsulation because it reduces the connections, which reduces the brain power to manage the connections, which makes programming easier. Classes also make for easier-to-maintain code when done right; but that does involve careful planning during design.

That is especially important when you use inheritance in your classes. I once wrote a program for a GUI design tool, back when they were somewhat novel. So I created a class for each onscreen item, with a base class to do things like `Draw()`, `ConvertToCode()`, handle coordinate setting/getting, etc. Then each descendant class added their own specific handlers — a `Button` class drew a button, output data to create a button in code, etc. Ditto for `Label`, and `TextBox`, and so forth.

The benefit was obvious. If I wanted to add a new object, say, `Image`, I still had to write handlers, but once written, they would naturally be called as needed — the code would call `Draw()`, and the appropriate handler drew something.

The alternative before classes was to create objects as data structures, and then use large switch statements to process those structures. So for example I'd write

```
LABEL_ConvertToCode()
BUTTON_ConvertToCode()
TEXTBOX_ConvertToCode()
```

Then add a function `ConvertToCode()` that would take a flag and switch to each of these; so the structures would each need this flag as well. And changes? I'd have to edit each and every switch statement, every time.

C++ hides all that — I still write `ConvertToCode()`, but now make it pure virtual, which forces the programmer to add a class handler. In turn, their `ConvertToCode()` child function for each object does whatever specifically is needed. Maintenance is easier, since adding classes involves much less infrastructure to edit (like the previous switches). And coding is easier, since I can work with the overall structure of the program using the parent classes, and let the children classes do their thing when their time comes.

But inheritance is a double-edged sword. For example, let's say I decide to write a `Line` class. But a mathematical line has length and no thickness, so what do `GetWidth()` and `GetHeight()` really return? I fudge — now `GetWidth()` and `GetHeight()` refer to the onscreen sizes only, and if for some reason I need real world line sizes, I'll have to cobble together a class for `GetRealSizeX()` and `GetRealSizeY()`. But for a line it's really `GetLength()`, which is nonstandard to the rest of the program, and so "breaks" my nice class layout. Sigh.

Another example is timers. A timer has no actual size, and doesn't need to be drawn, so now what? Again, a kludge can be used, but we're moving away from "pure" inheritance, and more into the "whatever gets it shipped" coding.

In my experience, I've found the best way to handle this is preparation and planning:

• Get as many of the details needed for class design in advance, so there's fewer last minute add-ons to break code.

• Plan classes with minimal interfaces. The fewer functions you need, the fewer you'll need to change in the future.

• The better you can analyze the problem, the more likely you'll pick the proper functions in advance. While especially important for classes that inherit (where all the attention is focused on a few key interface routines) it also applies to OOP in general.

If this sounds negative, it isn't: Object-oriented programming makes it far easier to solve many problems, and I recommend you learn to treat all your data as objects. It fits naturally with the way we think, and when done right, makes for easier to understand code — and easier to maintain code.

#22: Brand Everything

This is such a simple Tip, but I've been rewarded so often for using it in my code that it deserves its own point: Use special IDs and version numbers, and "brand" everything and anything:

• For every object or datum or whatever you create, add a unique ID key value to it. And for permanent objects like files, ALWAYS add a version number somewhere.

• Version branding makes upgrading easier since you know exactly what format you started with, every time (and you do change the version number each time you change the file format, right?) There's a reason version numbers are everywhere — they let you zero in on a specific set of code for troubleshooting, maintenance, feature sets and so on.

• Keys also make code easier/faster. Comparing for equals/not equals can be a simple as comparing keys. Especially when working with strings or classes, this can make a real time difference.

• Have every object get a unique key from a key generator, fancy talk for a variable that provides a unique ID, and then is incremented afterwards to get a new ID for the next object. I've already discussed this code in the tip about statics, but here's a general C function usable anywhere:

```
unsigned long GetUniqueID()
{
    static unsigned long key=1;
    return key++;
}
```

• One warning about using this technique: If your objects are stored permanently (like in a file), then you'll need to make sure the object IDs are always lower than the current counter value when you read them back in. Otherwise, you run the risk of duplicating IDs. I generally avoid all that by reassigning IDs to the objects as I read them back in, using a new (low) generator value. Another option is to read all the IDs in, noting the largest value, and then when done set the unique id value (key) to this number, plus one.

#23: Better, Faster, Stronger — The Basics

Performance tuning of code is a "full book" topic, so we can only cover the basics here and in the next tip — but even that will make a difference:

• Understand speed isn't everything. Take interpreted versus compiled. Java, C#, Visual Basic, PHP, and many other languages are interpreted, whereas ones like

C/C++ are compiled. Yet look at how much quality software is programmed with these interpreted languages. Computers are fast, and can take a bit of sluggishness in code, so don't get too wrapped up in teasing every bit of speed out of them.

• In line with this, a famous computer scientist (Donald Knuth) once said "premature optimization is the root of all evil." We think we're good at catching performance issues, but we often aren't. Program it first, and then attack the bottlenecks.

I once wrote a database reader that cached the whole DB into memory and so was very fast — once it was loaded. However, the loading, with no exaggeration whatsoever, was the single worst disappointment in the entire history of computing. I took the code home, tore it apart, and realized I was sorting each time I read a record in, guaranteeing that the list was always available in sorted order. So I scrapped that; instead, I read everything in at once, and then sorted a single time. The performance issue was resolved, and the reader went on to be useful for years.

• Know the balance. In C/C++ you can save a teeny-tiny bit of time by not initializing a variable. You can also spend an enormous amount of time debugging code that accidentally used that uninitialized variable's random value. Based on that, is the time benefit worth it? This is the kind of decision you'll hit when you write code — sometimes the fastest code is actually a bad trade-off, all things considered.

• Use profiling tools. Someday you will need to improve performance in your code, so get comfortable with some tools now. At a minimum you need to be able to measure a section of code before and after changes, to see if a fix made a difference. Even a timer started before a section of code, and then checking the time after, is better than nothing. Get used to how to do that on your system, and be ready.

• Be aware of lies, damned lies, and statistics. Many languages hide low level details from you nowadays, so "perfect" measurements may be a thing of the past. For instance, many interpreted languages actually compile behind the scenes, but only when the code is first executed. The result is the first run through can be slower, but the next one and subsequent ones are faster. As well, these compiled code caches get full and are occasionally flushed to make room for more, so code may run fine for awhile, and then slow down again in the future.

• The language designer's "average performance" for code is just that — an average. Garbage collection is a one example of this, doing well most times, then suddenly slowing down at the worst time performance-wise (at least it always seems the worst time!) You do have choices: Rewrite your code in a compiled language, rewrite just key portions in a compiled language, avoid opaque features like garbage collection (not easy!), or dig deep into your language's options to manage performance hits, such as by triggering a garbage collection just before time-critical work.

• Remember that performance math is confusing! Say you take X seconds running a function. You cut X by 50%, so the program is twice as fast, right? Sounds good, but the rest of the program's functions take time, too. For example, let's say a timing is ten seconds all together for a section of code, with your routine taking two seconds of that. You double its speed (or halve the time) so it takes one second, thereby saving you a second, for a 200% gain. Yahoo! But that just means the whole code section takes nine seconds instead of ten, with the overall gain at about 11% — still good, but not as earthshaking as it first appeared.

These items highlight that performance tuning is a game of inches rather than yards. Now let's turn from general theory to specifics you can use in your programs.

#24: I Feel the Need, the Need for Speed (Unless This Phrase Is Trademarked, in Which Case I Just Have a Strong Preference for Going Faster)

I like speeding up code — I mean I REALLY like it. Give me a chance to profile code and tweak the speed, and I will. Ironically, I can spend a lot of time when the goal is saving time.

Oh well.

However, one thing code tuning has taught me over the years is that there are different kinds of speed in software development:

• Speed of learning and maintenance. I once saw a hack for swapping variables without using a third temporary variable:

```
x = y ^ x;
y = y ^ x;
x = y ^ x;
```

This XOR swap algorithm is simple to write, needs no third variable, and is (presumably) faster — but it's a bear to understand at first. So do you use it? Time spent in learning and maintaining exotic algorithms should be reserved for ones that aren't in the "hacky" realm. And unless I'm working with a processor that's very limited in space (like an Arduino micro-controller) the usual temporary variable version works fine, and is much easier to understand.

• Speed of optimization. Have a one-off program or section of code that you rarely need to run, and even then for only minutes at a time? Then how much time do you invest in optimizing it? Likely that's time better spent elsewhere.

• Speed of code. While we want to write code fast, understand it and maintain it fast, this is the key — whenever possible, have it run faster.

So what to do? The trick is to understand the obvious stuff and practice coding it right until it's second nature:

• Do it yourself only when you have to. For example, if you need to manage 10,000,000 memory chunks each 128 bytes long, write your own memory manager in C++ and you'll quite likely get far better performance than (say) a Java or C# general memory garbage collector. But if your program is typical, memory needs vary, so don't expect to get much benefit from rolling your own. Plus you'll waste a lot of time finding that out.

• Think of memory levels as speed levels. For most people, this starts in the function level (unless you're doing assembly code, where you can access registers for even more speed). Local stack variables are faster than memory (heap) variables. Memory variables are faster than disk files. Disk is faster than the local network. The local network is (generally) faster than the cloud. And so on. Remember you can easily go an order of magnitude as you move down this list, so try to avoid the next step if you can (sometimes it's hard, for example if you don't have a large stack and need large local variables; then you're stuck and will have to use the heap).

• Cache rather than regenerate. Store a copy, and reuse it when needed instead of creating anew. One example of this is with lookup tables. Unless you've got a large object that has to be moved to slower memory to make room (like to a slower disk file), this often makes sense. Of course, the extra management can add time, so it might only be useful in the most time-critical situations.

• Lazy evaluations are great. Deferring work that might never be needed, such as placing variable creation inside an `if()`, costs zero time until used. Unless you absolutely need a value, consider only generating it when required and not before. Remember, the fastest code is the code never executed.

• Buffering takes time. Buffers are often a performance benefit, smoothing out I/O with the operating system. Most times they are fine and solve the problem simply. But if you need real speed, unbuffered I/O can sometimes dramatically improve throughput.

• Perception is key. I remember a story of a person brought in to program an elevator's movement, because people were complaining of elevator wait times. There's a lot of fancy algorithmic ways to handle the elevator's travel, but none are perfect, and ultimately someone will always be left waiting too long, and unhappy. His solution? Install a mirror in the lobby. Elevators took the same time, but people had something to do during the wait, so complaints went down. Likewise, no program's progress bar has ever sped up the program, but they've made the wait more tolerable.

#25: Strings Only Pretend to Be Your Friend

People never seem to catch on just how terrible strings are.

Yes, they are vital. And extremely useful. But they come with a huge performance hit. For almost every language, strings require a huge amount of time for the program or operating system to find a chunk of memory large enough to fit the string (I actually believe it's ALL languages, but there may be an exotic one that has tamed strings somehow, so I can't speak in absolutes). Not only that, but the code/OS must keep the remaining space in some kind of order: If you get too many big chunks and not enough "gaps" in the remaining memory to fit new strings (called fragmentation) you can have memory, memory everywhere, but none of it fit to use (bonus points for mangling a Sam Coleridge quote into a computer science book!)

For strings, there are several things to be specifically aware of when coding:

• Understand the penalty of string creation. As previously discussed, a string needs to call the operating system (or program code) to carve out a chunk of memory that can vary significantly in size from string to string. That takes time, much more than integer creation, for example, which is always a fixed size.

• Beware of string concatenation. Imagine splicing strings together. The result is bigger, so it likely needs a new, larger place to be stored. Finding that spot is time consuming. But there's more: Say you're doing a lot of concatenation, adding a character to the end of a string repeatedly, like reading in data from a file. Think of what is created as you read data in, and your string reaches 1,000 characters. The first string is zero length, then the next is 1, the next 2, etc. The next one is 3 characters, but has left behind both a 1 and 2 character string. The fourth? It's 4 characters, leaving behind 1+2+3=6 character's worth of strings. And 1,000? You've used and discarded 1+2+3+4+...+998+999 or 499,500 characters of data. That's 1/2 meg of memory waiting to be cleaned up!

Now, many languages try to make this faster. In .NET there is a StringBuilder, which lets you create the full-size string at once so it doesn't need to be relocated each time. C/C++ can do the same. Also, many string classes add a bit of extra space in memory behind each string when created, so adding a character or two won't always trigger a string copy. Nonetheless, it pays to be aware of it. One possibility is to keep the parts separate rather than concatenating them: On occasion, I've kept intermediate strings around, and combined them at the end of the function, just before returning.

• Fear garbage collection. Didn't use a StringBuilder or C array for that string? Then your 1,000 character string used a lot of intermediate strings, and they all need to go. That's where garbage collection comes in. In .NET languages and other interpreted languages like Java, a background routine looks for unused strings and removes them, them pushes everything remaining closer together to free up bigger chunks of space. This takes a lot of CPU cycles to do, and can hurt program performance if it comes at the wrong time. And it's not perfect (some items can't be moved, for instance), so you might still end up with a fragmentation problem. In C/C++ you have the much faster `delete` or `free()` to clean up memory, but then you'll need to handle the empty spaces yourself; otherwise, your memory becomes

Swiss cheese, and eventually no one spot will be big enough for your next piece of data. For other languages like PHP, you won't be running long, so hopefully the memory you use will be fine (although there is garbage collection since PHP 5.3).

The moral of the story? Strings are different beasties from other variables, because they come in all sizes. As a result, if your program gets big and busy, you might hit against some limits when using them. Thinking about strings like a computer does will give you some insight into what may or may not be slowing down your program.

#26: Threads, Twelve Step Programs, and Grey Hairs

Should you use threads?

Should you use GOTO?

These are questions that promote a lot of acrimony, so I will skip the religious war and state what I've found: Threads are the crack cocaine of the programming world, and you have to watch getting hooked when using them.

Too harsh? OK — but I have my reasons to be scared of threads.

I once worked on a program where the previous developer had threaded some download code. Perfectly fine. But he had to access the GUI to show the progress. Only he couldn't, since (as with many languages) the GUI ran on a separate thread that was prevented from talking with other threads, to avoid synchronization issues.

Fine; so he then used the language-approved way to talk between threads. But he needed still more GUI communication, so buried in his thread code was a pointer to the GUI data he needed. However, that pointer was not accessed in the language-approved way to talk between threads. And occasionally he called that pointer at the wrong time, with the result that very, very rarely, an incredibly hard to reproduce bug blew up the display.

Time and time again I've found that threads cause very subtle but very bad issues if you're not careful:

• Threading is zero-tolerance programming. You MUST understand threads thoroughly to program them. You need to understand mutexes, semaphores, locking and racing conditions, atomic operations — in fact, everything to do with threads working together politely (lumped under the equally polite term "thread-safe.") The reason is that threads can preempt at any time, and things we take for granted stop making sense.

For example, let's take our favorite unique-ID code in a slightly contrived example:

```
unsigned long N=gSeedUniqueID;
gSeedUniqueID++;
return N;
```

Imagine two threads, each racing to get their own unique id at almost the same time. The first grabs the value of `gSeedUniqueID` into `N` (let's say 1) but before it can increment `gSeedUniqueID` the next thread takes over. It too grabs `gSeedUniqueID` — which is still 1 — and goodbye unique ids (this by the way is the definition of a race condition, where two threads race to do something and, without proper thread protection, get in each other's way).

Now you might think the chance of them tripping over each other in exactly this way is highly unlikely. Yes, but not impossible. And that is the problem. Usually it's clear sailing with no conflict between threads. But what if just once in a million, or two million, or even a hundred million calls it actually does do that: How on earth do you test, or reproduce the bug? The only solution is to build it right the first time. And that means zero tolerance for threads unless you know how to program them properly, so crack open the computer science books on this one.

• Threads are messy to debug. Thread interactions are arguably as close to truly random as we can get on the computer, and random bugs are notorious to debug. Look at the previous example: Interrupt just before or just after these statements and the code is perfectly reasonable and does what it's supposed to. But sooner or later those threads could switch at just the right spot to mess up the code. It may take milliseconds, or hours, or years. Or never happen even if the code runs for a billion centuries. Ordinary bugs are hard enough to find — why create ones that are almost impossible to catch?

• Threads are seductive and addictive (this is the "crack cocaine" part). Let's face it, none of this would be a problem if threads were uninteresting; people would avoid using them. But they are so useful and interesting. Who doesn't want to "send off" code to have it magically process on its own, or send time-consuming code off to a thread so your GUI stays responsive? And you should use them for your programs, with these caveats: Make your code thread-safe, and understand that any interaction with the "outside" (outside of the thread that is) MUST be analyzed for potential thread problems.

You can use threads properly, but be forewarned they are addictive, with some major side effects if not managed properly. So always thread with care, and be thread-safe.

#27: Threading Your Way Through Threads Safely

So you read the previous tip, nodded your head, agreed with everything, then said to yourself "I think I'm going to go program some threads now."

Sigh.

OK, I can't blame you, but please take a moment to think about threading before you get in too deep.

The fact is, threads are perfectly fine in isolation. If you use a thread to read a file by itself, process its data, and return a result, then you've got a great thread, a safe thread, an easy to test and debug and maintain thread. (Although with one teeny-tiny bugaboo: The thread has to anticipate the program closing early, so even this isn't a perfect example of a thread in isolation.)

But few threads are like that. Sooner or later someone will want it to provide a status update, or interact with the outside world in some other way. And like I mentioned, even stopping the thread is an issue — what if the thread is doing some complex file manipulation at the time of stopping?

The fact is, most threads have to communicate and synchronize, and that's where the computer-sciency stuff comes in:

• Atomic. Derived from the little bits of matter we all know and love, the term is based on the ancient Greek word for indivisible (ironically, atoms ARE divisible; maybe we should have just said "indivisible" for threads). The point is, an atomic operation is an operation that is all in one; never half done, either never started or else completely finished. Some atomic operations are easy, like reading and writing Booleans — they are either true or false. This is because in every system I've encountered, a Boolean is stored in one chunk of memory, and the processor reads or writes that whole chunk as a single piece — atomically.

In contrast, integers and floats are usually not atomic. If one thread interrupts another thread while a shared number is written out, the second thread may get a partially written value (which we define technically as "crap"). Even here there is low-tech help: Every computer you'll likely encounter writes a byte (8 bits) as a single operation, making it atomic. So besides Booleans, you can read and write values from 0-255 without thread problems.

Writing a single byte is one thing: Full-fledged coordination between threads so they don't get in each other's way really requires you to call in the big guns for atomic operations: The operating system will need to step in and manage things. That leads us to the operating system constructions:

• Mutexes. Short for MUTually EXclusive, this is a bit of code that makes sharing safe and atomic. Say you have two threads needing to open a log file and write

---

some data to its end. Either one can go first, but like two big guys trying to go through a door together, they MUST go one at a time. A mutex is like a uniquely numbered ticket given to each of these gentlemen. If their number is next, they go. If not, they wait and check back from time to time — comfortable in the knowledge that when it's their turn no one will push past them.

• Semaphores. Now we know how to share a single door. What if there's more than one door? Or to make it more practical (or at least grosser), a big bowl of ice cream and two spoons? Assuming that no one has a problem with sharing spoons and bowls, the problem for those filthy folk is that there may not be enough spoons (tools) for everyone to access the ice cream (resources). If there was only one spoon, a mutex would work: I got it or I wait around until it's available. But that ice cream is melting fast, so you want everyone eating as quickly as possible, with both spoons in use. You need a semaphore.

Now instead of locking/unlocking a single number to go through a door, people (threads) check for a count of available items. When a spoon is available, they grab it. But you see the problem — now you need control over who gets to grab it first, and that adds more complexity. And what if they don't want to hang around until it's available (I mean, sure it's ice cream, but people have lives to live). Then you need a way to contact them (or for threads, possibly waking them up) so they grab a spoon, have their fill, and then end their turn and let the next ice cream lover get a chance.

One way to do this is to use a number system (like mutexes) where each person gets a number and the next valid number goes. As you can imagine, in the computer world this can get tricky — as we saw earlier, what if two threads ask for a number at almost the same time and get the same one? So semaphores need atomic operations as well (is your head spinning yet?)

• Starvation and deadlocks. Dessert is over; time for the main course (doesn't everyone eat dessert first?) Now you have five friends sitting in front of five bottomless bowls of spaghetti. It sounds like everyone can concentrate on their own meal and nothing bad will happen, right? Not so fast. This is slippery spaghetti, and the only way to eat it is with two forks. And unfortunately, the Bottomless Spaghetti House has only provided five forks (doubtless to discourage pursuing the "bottomless" part of the meal). Since simple math tells us that only 2.5 friends can eat at a time, and integer math tells us we really mean only 2, what do we do?

Part of the problem is made easier for us, because our friends wax loquacious often, philosophizing on anything and everything. So while three talk, two other "philosophers" can eat. But sooner or later, three will want to dine at the same time. They will pick up one fork, pick up another — and be one short. What does that third person do? Put the fork down and try again, and maybe go hungry if everyone else has quicker reflexes? Or keep the fork and wait for a second one, which leads to a problem, since soon everyone else tries that, and then everybody has one fork, and nobody eats.

I'll avoid the suspense: Like the ice cream dilemma earlier, our dining philosophers can use semaphores to solve the problem. "Dining philosophers" is in fact a half-century old thought experiment that led to semaphores — feel free to look it up for more details. But the key here is that when a thread (or really anything that has to share politely) needs two or more resources, there's a potential problem if those resources are not all immediately available: Starvation (if everyone else keeps grabbing the forks) or Deadlock (if everyone holds on to one fork while waiting for the second). And these are common issues for most threads, since they usually need to share multiple resources with other threads.

• Naughtiness. So at this point your code is thread-safe (which by the way is what "thread-safe" is all about, the promise that your code can be safely run amongst multiple threads, without ever getting in each other's way). But what if it isn't? Perhaps there's a bug. Say a thread grabs a mutex, and then never gives it back. Everyone thinks the thread is still in the bathroom, but it's gone home, and is reading a paper and sipping coffee, with the bathroom key, I mean mutex, still in its pocket. Meanwhile, there's a lot of angry threads waiting to use the can...

Or perhaps you've got code where the programmer didn't understand or just ignored the polite world of threadsafedom, taking resources as needed, and risking a breakdown ("I have to wait for a mutex? No way — I only need it for like a microsecond. So here I go, what's the worst that could happen...?") A mutex is useless for control if even one thread refuses to follow the rules. This is a real risk with threading, programming that doesn't or won't abide by the rules. About all you can do in that case is rewrite or gut that code, because living with it is NOT an option.

OK, by now you've got an idea of how polite threading works, and hopefully an idea of how hard it is to get it "just right." Now I beg of you, crack open that computer science textbook, and study threading properly, and in detail. You, and all the programmers working with your future code, will be grateful that you did.

#28: Code Migration: Ready for Any "Port" in a Storm

Perhaps one day you will have a need or desire to get your code out to more people, on different computers/devices. Maybe you wrote a fun program you want more people to use (or even pay for); maybe your boss wants to get more market share; maybe you just want the brain-expanding challenge of compiling Doom and running it on a Raspberry PI (too late!)

But no matter your reasons, moving the code to new and different machines means you'll need to learn about porting to do it. And the key to moving code from one computer system to another is preparation:

• Data size. Take a simple example: If you coded a program in iOS and used "int" throughout, then ported it to Visual BASIC 6 (I said simple example, not realistic) you'd likely have it blow up spectacularly. For many, many reasons of course, but one specific one is that in the VB6 world an `int` is 16 bits long, whereas for iOS it is currently 64 bits. 64 bits is roomy for values; 16 bits is cramped, and code breaks in interesting ways (for example, if you pass a function +32768 the 16-bit world converts it to -32768).

One solution is to specify the exact size you want using `int8_t`, `uint32_t` and the like. Or even ones like `uint_fast16_t` or `int_least32_t` which try for the more speed-efficient and space-efficient variables, respectively. But that's only if your compiler supports these C++ version 11 options, which brings up another problem of porting, tools.

• Your tool chain. You are at the mercy of two compilers: The one you started on and the one you are porting to. This gives you two possible pain points.

I recently had a hugely annoying problem working with the Android NDK (for C++) and porting code to it. Google recently moved from their own build tool ndk-build to the standard cmake. One benefit is that cmake is a popular tool, and learning it is easier since there's plenty of documentation. So the problem was, do I port that code to the current system and then move everything to cmake somewhere down the line, or learn cmake and do a single, more complicated, port? Either way, I had extra work, plus I felt I was tap-dancing to their tune (and I really don't like to tap dance). With porting, you're potentially dancing double speed, for two compiler environments. So keep alert for unexpected changes.

• Your compiler. Every compiler has an annoying collection of dross that you have to manage to build your program. This is especially the case with things like non-standard compiler directives; `#define` macros and the like. My advice? Work hard to minimize how much platform-dependent code you need to change, and then keep it very localized. Use standard methods to wrap non-standard code, and document it like crazy. One file of conditionals sure beats sweeping all the code for every change whenever you port.

• Write portable code from the beginning. I recently ported some code to write to a graphic (bitmap) in C. Fundamentally, every bitmap can be viewed as a two-dimensional array of bits, so the actual conversion code was simple and fast. The hardest part was the OS-specific issues of setting up a bitmap and passing it to the call. The final solution was to write the OS-portable bit-twiddling routine as a separate function from the OS-specific bitmap creation code — something I wish I had separated out when I first wrote it, back when it was on a familiar OS/compiler...

• Avoid assumptions. Like the bitmap code, we often assume the way it's done is generic until we port and find out our new environment doesn't quite support that. So take time to plan by reading up on how things are done in other operating systems. For example, take human languages: Windows has very good support for languages in Unicode, but not all of that is portable elsewhere. At one time Unicode was the salvation for internationalizing text, but now UTF-8 is the front runner, due in no small part to its popularity on the Web. The key then? If you program right from the start with UTF-8 support in your user-visible strings, porting should go much easier.

Assumptions can be very tricky because, by definition, we aren't thinking about exceptions. For example, a pointer refers a specific spot in the computer's memory. So of course, comparing two pointers should always tell you if they're referring to the same or different locations, right? Not so fast. In the old days 8086 chips (the great granddaddies of our Intel processors) used segments, so a pointer consisted of a segment and an offset, which were combined together to form the final address. As you can imagine, with two parts there were multiple ways to specify a particular address, and care was needed when comparing pointers.

Ancient history? Not if you get into micro-controller devices like the Arduino, which uses something called Harvard architecture, where a pointer to program memory is NOT the same as a pointer to data memory! So whenever possible, try to question any assumptions you have before you port code, and confirm if they are the same on the destination system.

• Abstract code. Say you want to talk to another program. You could use TCP, a memory-mapped file, OLE, smoke signals, or any number of options. But what if first you move the communication calls to an API, for example, `SendString()` and `ReceiveString()` to do the job? Now your whole program can use these two functions, and you don't even have to decide on the internals yet! This way, you can do OS-specific communication if you want, and swap in a better/different option later when you port. But if your code is full of implementation-specific calls scattered around, the porting could require a lot of editing.

• Eschew Obfuscation [Avoid complication]. Use a fancy trick to solve a problem in one computer, and I'm guessing the chance is high it won't port easily. Maintenance can be a problem too. And no guarantee of benefits, either. Take the XOR swap hack I mentioned earlier: Today's processors try to parallelize instructions, which is harder (and therefore slower) with the XOR trick than the "ordinary" way of using a temporary variable. In the end, good generic code with very small nonportable sections (if absolutely needed) is the easiest to port.

In short — plan ahead as much as possible. First peek over the fence, and you'll have a better idea what the neighborhood looks like when you do go through the gate.

#29: IDE Should Stand for "I Don't Expect (To Program Without It)," or Something Like That

You kids today have it so easy.

When I was young I coded C++ on Windows Notepad, and every day I had to walk 5 miles through chest-high snow to get to my computer — and was darn grateful for it!

Seriously though, when I compare what IDE (Integrated Development Environments) have become from the old days (last century) I am very, very happy. You should be too. Writing code in a text editor is not nearly as much fun as doing it with syntax coloring, built-in debugging, context-sensitive help, refactoring, and all those other programmer-ready features.

But it comes at a price: Programming+typing, versus programming+typing AND reading a user's manual. It's a testimony to how useful they are that I do recommend reading that manual. First thing though is to choose your IDE:

• Your work may mandate a specific program. If so, then your choice is simple: Theirs. Doesn't mean you can't learn another one at home, though.

• Your choice is also often limited by your compiling environment (computer), language, destination computer, and so on. I recommend going for the most popular one of these choices, since when you have questions (and you will have questions!) answers are easier to find online.

• Your future goals factor in. For example, if you plan to do cross-platform work, an IDE like Eclipse will mean that for the most part you'll learn things once, and then carry that knowledge across various operating systems. Likewise, if you are aiming to be an MS-Head or Apple Guru, then Microsoft or Apple tools are the appropriate options.

• How many programming languages do you use? Although most IDEs support multiple languages, some do it better than others. Ideally, you'll want one tool that supports all of your languages. But quality is so important that I'd recommend learning two or more IDEs that handle everything well for their individual languages, versus using one that does a "so-so" job of them all. The initial pain of learning new software is nothing compared to the steady grind of "oh yeah I can't do that here" every time you work with a different language on an awkward IDE.

Of course life is never simple. You may not get the best pick right now. For example, a while back Google/Android swapped their IDE from Eclipse to Android Studio — time to learn a second IDE, whether you wanted to or not! But pick something, and whatever you are working with, make it count by learning everything you can, especially:

• Debugging is vital. If I can set a breakpoint and view variables, 80% of my debugging needs are met. If I can view individual threads, change variable values, skip breakpoints conditionally (so I only stop at pass #345, for example) then life just keeps getting better and better.

• Syntax formatting and highlighting. I find syntax coloring is valuable for quickly moving through a file (where, for example, that big patch of forest green is commented-out code), but most importantly I need to edit it. I like my braces a specific way (Allman style, if you must know), and if I set it in the IDE, I get a second benefit: My code formatter will reformat other's code to show it that way. Same with tabs: I hate them so much that I turn them into 2 spaces and then set "Convert tabs to spaces" on every editor I use — immediately. Like sitting in a brand new chair versus one you've already broken in, your code benefits from having your environment set up the way you're comfortable with ASAP.

• Code tweaking. Getting your code reformatted is great. Easily changing it is even better. I'm a huge fan of refactoring. Simple example: Recently, I was trying to decide whether a variable should be called recID (a unique identifier for a database record) or cutID (since each DB record points to an audio cut). After some back and forth, I decided that recID made more sense object-wise (objectively?), and with that realization, I could refactor/rename the variable everywhere using my IDE, quickly, and without making a mistake (unlike search and replace, with its blind string replacement accidentally changing parts of other variable names). It's also handy when I want to turn a public variable into a private one with setter/getter functions — and many more uses besides. If there's one feature you'll want to understand well, this is it.

• Syntax popups. Called a lot of different things, you can start typing something and the editor pops up suggestions. Use it to learn exotic parts of the language, or to just write code faster. For example, is that function `SetMaxWidth()` or `set_max_width()`? Type it and see. Keeping those details straight can be brain-wearying, so let the computer do it.

Go pick an IDE, fire it up, and work through the options — you'll be amazed how much your productivity improves as you learn it.

#30: A Workman's/Workwomen's/Workperson's Code Is Only as Sharp as His/Her/Their Tools

As a programmer, an IDE is your most vital tool. But there are many others that will make programming easier and more enjoyable, and help you become a more well-rounded developer to boot. Here's a few I use:

• Text editor. A word processor won't hack it for most programming tasks. Usually you are working with ASCII or Unicode or similar, and a word processor wants to "tweak" the results for you. Not good. At the very least, it will take your lines and wrap them around on the display into paragraphs!

In contrast, a line editor preserves the characters of content, and lets you work with them in a text-based way (no auto-correction, for instance). Ideally, you want one that includes regular expressions, which gives you a handy way to massage text easily, as the earlier tip on regular expressions pointed out. Large file loading and long line loading is a bonus, since you can come across really big text files in your work (like SQL dumps). I use psPad, but an Open Source version some prefer is Notepad++.

• Word processor. Text editor for text, and a word processor for when you need to communicate with people. Spell checking, grammar checking, auto-correct — they mean others can read your words instead of asking "what is he saying?" Many people use a Microsoft product, but I'm a fan of OpenOffice, and lately its offshoot LibreOffice.

• Spreadsheet. Need to work with numbers and dates? A spreadsheet is a free-form editor for numbers. Get used to one, and you'll find yourself going back to it frequently for problems a text editor just can't solve easily. For example, I use it when I need to create a numbered list. Paste the items into one column, and add another column with numbers (in LibreOffice Calc, just enter a 1 in a cell, and then click and drag the cell corner down to fill the rest of the column with 2, 3, 4, etc). Copy and paste a comma down a column between the two and also after the last column, then copy the whole block to have a numbered array for your program.

• Difference program. You have a source file from last week — what changes did you make since then? Load it and the current file into a difference program and visually see what's changed. Useful any time you have text files that might differ. I use WinDiff.

• Browser. You probably have a favorite. I recommend downloading them all, since likely you'll do something web-based at one point in time or another, and you'll want to check for rendering differences on each. A key advantage is if you set one browser to forget everything on closing down (cookies, URLs, history, etc); then you can test a web page as a "brand new" visitor over and over again, something you can't really do with your favorite browser.

• Virtual computer and drive. Virtual drives let you set up individual test beds that can be wiped and reloaded on a whim. Especially if you work with free operating systems like Linux or FreeBSD, by combining them with a virtual CPU you have a powerful and secure way to test products in a "fresh" new OS each and every time. They're also handy when you need to run an old program that won't work anymore (like 16-bit programs after Windows XP). I use VirtualBox.

• grep. Short for "globally search a regular expression and print" it uses regular expressions to scan files for matches. Think of it as a text file scanner with regular expressions. A lot of programming tasks get easier when you can set grep loose, say on a directory to find an obscure reference, or where in which file you called `printf()` and accidentally passed it the company name in all lower case...

• Graphics program. Chances are you are dealing with a graphical environment when programming, so expressing yourself graphically as well as programmatically makes you a double threat. Roughly speaking, there's two types of graphics programs: Raster (pixel based) and vector (line or shape based). Raster programs let you get things pixel-perfect, and are invaluable for designing items like icons. Vector programs, since their artworks are resolution independent, work best for designing objects that will need to be resized in many ways (like logos).

Combining the two for example, you'd use a vector program to design the initial program icon, and a raster program to tweak each individual resized version to look best at its specific resolution.

But that just scratches the surface, since once you start working with a graphics program, you'll see many ways you can use it to do your own design work. And because you aren't waiting on a design team, your software turnaround (and productivity) will increase.

Although I've used Corel products for years (CorelDraw for vectors, Paintshop-Pro for raster), many people are fond of Adobe products. For the price conscious, Paint.NET is a good raster art program, as is Gimp, and Inkscape is well regarded for vector graphics.

• Local server. I use XAMPP, which lets me easily set up a test web server on my Windows machine. When you do even the minimum of web file edit & upload & tweak & redit & reupload, you get very tired of the cycle. A local tool lets you edit in place and just refresh a local web page on your browser. When I do work on software like WordPress plugins or JavaScript, it makes a huge difference in productivity.

• Problem specific tools. This grab bag includes tools I use for particular projects. For example, when I need to get a complicated regular expression "just right," I use RegEx Coach; a programmer's calculator for bit and hexadecimal conversions (usually a setting in the calculator that your OS provides); a good color chart for palette design (search online for "palette online" to find a wide variety); a timer for monitoring my paid work (again, a quick search online, or roll your own — they are easy and fun to write); a to-do list (I use the now-defunct Ecco, but a "to-do.txt" file on your computer will work fine).

• Music player. Talk to any programmer worth his or her salt, and they will tell you that you often need to tune things out. Earphones and a good playlist can really help with work. Music moves, and a "power playlist" can energize, classical can soothe, even nature sounds may help. Have a variety of playlists handy, get a quality pair of headphones (or speakers if you can play music out loud in your workplace) and see if your productivity doesn't increase. Although there are many choices, I'm fond of foobar2000 for Windows.

This is just a sampling of the tools you may find useful. Take the time to try out a few and really learn them well. As they say, to the person who has a hammer, everything looks like a nail. But to the person with a hammer, screwdriver, crowbar, drill, chisel — you get the idea — everything looks exactly like it is, a problem waiting for the right tool to fix it. Be that person.

Discipline — The 20 In 80/20

Although the Pareto principle has been butchered over the years (the original observation was that 80% of the land was owned by 20% of the people in Italy), it reminds us that everything is unevenly concentrated — even programming. But if the goal is to focus on the 20% that matters, then you'll get more results with less effort using these tips.

#31: Don't Solve the Problem Too Soon

We're all guilty of it — someone is talking to us and we go "a-ha, um, yes, here's what to do…" Basically, we're giving the answer even as they are still stating the problem.

The average human can think a lot faster than the average human can speak — about 3X faster according to one estimate. I suppose that's why people seem to believe that while person A is speaking, person B has "heard it all" about 1/3rd of the way through! Of course that's ridiculous, but it highlights that we need to slow down when it comes to listening.

We also need to slow down in analyzing a problem, for several reasons:

• Complex ideas need time to absorb. Complex ideas make us uncomfortable. That's why everyone wants elevator pitches — short, pithy sentences that describe things. The movie E.T. is "stranded alien needs help from boy to get home." So why did the movie take months to film and cost millions of dollars? Because the initial description only hinted at the complexity. Make no mistake: An elevator pitch gets interest and a foot in the door, but when it comes to problem solving, you need detailed analysis, something you can't do without time.

• You may be tempted to settle on an answer too quickly. Take the time to explore other options, and they might provide superior solutions. One reason there are so many programming languages is that each has a focus. For example, Visual Basic has a reputation for easy solutions to simple problems, whereas C/C++ is tied to high performance. Rust, to safety. Erlang, fault-tolerant real time processing. And so on. If a different language can give you a different insight into how to solve a problem, isn't it obvious that there may be other factors that can make the problem easier, things you need to examine first?

• You look bad. We've all seen the show where the genius answers what the person was thinking before they've finished — perfectly. What they don't show is real life where your answer is really, really off the mark, and the client wonders just how low your IQ is. Looking smart once in a hundred times is not worth looking stupid the other ninety-nine.

Are there exceptions? Of course, like the elevator pitch, getting out there with a solution quickly can get a project the green light, or make you look super-smart at a key moment. But generally speaking, most times you will want to wait and think — a lot — before answering with a solution.

#32: Lose the Attitude, Find a New One, or Just Make It Better

Let's be honest: Ego is a huge part of coding. We all think we are the best, but as Highlander says, "there can be only one" (and so sorry to everyone else, but it's me).

I knew a fellow who I suppose was a good programmer (he definitely thought so), but was a mess to deal with. Ask him a question and you got a snarky reply. On forums he was the kind to mock people when they didn't understand something right away — and I mean really mock them (sadly, that type seems to be increasingly common). The takeaway? I would never work with that person. And I'm not alone. So how effective is he as a programmer if no one wants to work with him?

Here is a truism about programming:

The best programmers don't have to brag or mock.

Really good programmers don't have to tell everyone how good they are at something. They also don't have to pick on others to make themselves feel better. They have respect for others because they are good, they don't have to prove anything, and they can be sympathetic to newbies instead of always feeling challenged by others.

How do you get to be a really good programmer?

By caring about it, a lot:

• Force yourself to try new things software-wise. Learn new languages. Read other's comments and articles and books on new techniques, and put that knowledge into practice.

• Be humble. After all, no matter how smart you are, there's smart people elsewhere, and any five of them can run circles around you (After all, even if you're twice as smart, there's five of them, with 5 times 24 hours a day to catch up. Do the math).

• Be diligent. No one can know everything. Even while your knowledge should be broadening, realize that depth in one or two key subjects is vital. People that have a shallow understanding of a bunch of things can't be anything more than "blue-sky" folk. Don't be one of them. Confidence and self-satisfaction comes from really digging into something and understanding it fully.

• Be proud. You're in this business to do good work. Take pride in well-crafted functions, good variable names, visually pleasing GUIs, fast performance, lean code, and everything else that makes a program great. To the craftsman, even changing a single variable name to correctly explain what it does is a source of pride, and a source of annoyance if it's inexact.

• Keep a sense of humor, since mistakes will happen. Overly serious people can get upset too easily. I once worked on a mainframe computer whose operating system let you view task status by entering a number from 0-9 (a maximum of ten tasks). Idly, I wondered what entering 10 would do. It turned out it crashed the system, and aborted a $20,000 data processing job that needed to be restarted. And while it wasn't exactly my fault (even the simplest OS code should have checked for values over 9!), I was mortified. My boss laughed it off, sent me home, and restarted the job again. I'll always be impressed by his attitude. Be that guy, and problems won't give you an ulcer.

• Be egoless. Sometimes work will feel like digging holes and filling them back in. The manager wants a boring job done, and done right now. The fun stuff is going to another staff member. You have to learn a language or tool that doesn't interest you. A test bed is irritating to run and finicky to work with. And so on. Here's a key point to remember: Your attitude makes the difference in each case, and in your career prospects. The great programmer sees it as a challenge, and tackles it positively. The poor programmer tries to get out of it, and can take twice as long to get a job done (or more). The benefit is that if you persevere even in the jobs no one wants, you build a reputation. And if work slows down, who will they want to keep: The jack-of-all trades who is ready to help anywhere, or the guy who disappears whenever the tough jobs come around?

• Be passionate — at something. I like solving problems. A lot. And when I have a chance to solve a software problem I am usually delighted. I want you to get the same kick out of what you do. Enjoy programming, and get better. Or get out. If software doesn't interest, please, I beg of you, find that job you'll want to do great work in! You have one life; why not look back and say "I did good work" instead of "Well, I kept busy."

Programming is a career — but for a great programmer, it's much, much more.

#33: Just Code It Right, Right From the Start, Right?

Quick programs are bad programs.

You know what I'm talking about. You want a proof of concept or just a fast program to do a job, so you leave off the extras. Like meaningful variable names. Or exception handling. Or good comments. Or any comments.

Maybe even a goto has snuck in there because you just wanted to get the code done NOW. So it runs, it does the job, and you put it away.

Then six months later you come across a problem and you think, hey, I wrote something to do that a while ago. You dig it out, run it, and then spend almost as long as it took to write it trying to understand it again.

Treasure those examples. That is a personalized-for-you case study in how not to write software. No theoretical example gets through as well as one you remember bringing on yourself (or, "experience is a good teacher").

I know I have lots of examples like that, mercifully fewer new ones as time goes by. When you have only yourself to blame, you realize it's up to you to stop it in the future:

• Read all this book and apply it. Seriously — I wrote it for a reason. Better software is one of them (buying my own island is another one, but I'm guessing better software is a tad more realistic).

• Watch the urge to overshoot. Fast code is sloppy code. Take a moment for the basics. Use meaningful variable and function names. Format your code. If a function quickly grows, take the time to tame it or break it up. Add comments on the stuff you're having trouble with, because dollars to doughnuts it'll really be an issue six months from now! In short, slow down and make sure you're got the current code in good shape before you rush on to the next section.

• Fit in some time for analysis. When you're done, take a bit of time to review your code. As I mentioned, an example like this is a great learning experience. What was the hard stuff to remember? Then that's the part that gets the comments. Would a better variable name or function name make sense? Then sweat over them in the future. Wished you'd saved that data as XML instead of a binary dump? Then that's where your time should be focused in the next program. And so on.

• Keep the smart-ass stuff for comedy routines. The computer language Python was named after the comedy troop. How long before the snickering subsides and it stops being funny (it's still better than Rust, whose name constantly reminds me that programs too can corrode, grow old, and die. Or Swift, which requires every one of my Internet searches to start with "swift programming language" unless I want to find out the latest in Taylor Swift's life). I once wrote an obfuscator that made variable names using "v" and "w": vvwwv, vwvww, vwwvww, etc. I went for hard to understand and confusing names deliberately, to make reverse engineering difficult. You want the opposite in your code, so do the opposite in coding, too. Skip the amusing variable names, insider jokes, Easter eggs, and other silliness. Like hearing a knock-knock joke after your age hits the double digits, the jokes fade, and eventually you're left with sadly oddball code that doesn't really help you understand the program.

• You'll likely reuse the code again, so plan now for that. Every non-trivial program has something interesting in it, a bit of code you'll consider reusing (I'm a huge believer in keeping code repositories of my "greatest hits" for reuse). As I've mentioned, if the code is bad, you'll spend a lot of time reworking it, so a teeny-tiny bit of extra work today can save huge amounts of effort tomorrow.

• Take a moment to learn. New code often includes a new area or two you might benefit from knowing better. An example for me a while back was XML. I was happy to keep using text files for data, but with so many readers and writers in different languages that processed XML, I felt it would be a more future-proof storage format. So on a project, I forced myself to add XML support. One semi-annoying project later, I had code that was easy to maintain, and written in a format widely understood; unlike my text files, which often required some explanation on how to parse them. With reuse, that extra time spent on learning can save you time on the next coding job. It seems counter-intuitive, but it's been proven true to me time and time again.

If I can emphasize anything, it's that bad code must die, or better yet, never be born. When you create something, make it good, and make it a habit to learn to write good code all the time. Your future self with thank you for it.

#34: Code Like You May Need to Change Things, 'Cuz You Likely Will

I think one of the best skills a programmer can have is to code with an eye to the future. Whether you write a "toy" program for your own use, or work on the company's flagship product, it will almost invariably change. Anticipating that change makes a huge difference on your workload in the future.

I once worked on a rewrite of a program for audio management. Ridiculously simple — just keep a list of songs in memory and make it available to the consumer in a pretty way. Any programmer worth his/her salt could hack together an internal array and solve the problem.

But looking forward, I went with SQL and a database solution. Why?

• An in-memory array is easy to program when it's 100 or 1,000 or even 10,000 items. But what if it gets to one million? Or ten million? How about multiple users? Now instead of adding more code (new features) you're constantly optimizing old code and bogging down in it. In contrast, scaling up with a database is often a case of just plugging in a more powerful server.

• I picked a specific database (sqlite) since it was royalty free and standard SQL, important points to me (yes, I'm talking about you, Microsoft!) It's also sup-ported by smartphones and tablets, so porting the code to Android and iOS would go easier/faster should that happen.

• Popularity also makes it easier to maintain. SQL is a popular language, and any search on "how to" in SQL generally returns plenty of answers. New features that require custom SQL are often just an online query or two away.

The result was that the extra time spent up front was repaid many-fold: As new features were added, less rewriting was needed.

So you're convinced — future-proofing your code makes sense — how then do you do it?

• Use the common denominator as much as possible. Take Microsoft browsers. For whatever reason, they added features no one else had, or tweaked the features to make them non-standard. For years, coding CSS and Javascript on the web involved coding two versions: One for Internet Explorer, and one for everyone else. But if you wanted to write code that worked everywhere, you simply used less features, and didn't try to push the envelope. Or looked for features that did most of what you wanted, and then just added a compartmentalized section of code to handle the dif-ferences. Fewer differences equaled less to change and maintain.

• Think open-ended whenever you can. Like my SQL example, choose the product that has growth potential. Ditto for algorithms. Anticipate where growth will lead, and try to provide that solution as much as possible/reasonable now.

• Strip out or lock out undefined behavior in code. How many times have you heard of someone using a bug in code to do something unusual? If it gets too popu-lar, a company can be forced to support a code mistake for a long, long time. So make sure code can do what it is specified to do, and only that.

• Assume as little as possible about the Operating System. Unicode makes for simple text programming, until you need to rewrite it for an Operating System that doesn't support it natively. All that display code will need reworking if you require a too-large minimum monitor size or color range (the decent computer running Win-dows in the 1990s had an 800 by 600 display with a 256-color display palette!) De-pending on a key feature of the Operating System may be necessary for your code, but if that feature changes or goes away, you're in a game of Crack the Whip — and guess who is going to crack first?

• If in doubt, leave it out. Think of it: Every feature should involve coding, code review, testing, documenting, and more. So every feature change should involve a repeat of those steps. In the end, a change in a program will be like herding elephants — slow and difficult to do. We need a certain number of features to please the sales department, but consider holding back the less-interesting ones if you can. A useful method is to test the program with real users: If a feature doesn't rock them, carefully evaluate if you want to maintain that ho-hum feature for years to come.

• If you push the envelope expect to get licked a lot (envelope, licked — get it?) People who are on the bleeding edge BLEED; that's why it's called "bleeding edge." A while back, Swift was trying to gain traction in Apple's world over Objective-C. But it frequently changed major parts of its language, resulting in massive rewrites for any programmer trying to work in it. Ouch. It's not the only language that is rapidly evolving (Rust comes to mind) but frankly, I'd rather program in Objective-C a few more years, and then switch to Swift when it finally stabilizes. I can't waste my time learning, then unlearning and relearning; I need to program for a living. My time is valuable, and yours should be too. Of course, ignore this if your company is paying you to take the time to learn!

#35: Inoculate Yourself Against NIH Syndrome

You can code a great Binary Search, can't you? Linked list? So why not write your own code all the time?

It's called Not Invented Here Syndrome (NIH) and happens when programmers don't want to use other packages or solutions, whether a custom package from another company or off-the-shelf components.

It's not a perfectly clear-cut issue, so here are some pros and cons:

• Pro: Be an early adopter and get rewards! The first people to jump on the Apple iPhone bandwagon had a wide-open field and an advantage. Sure, you had to learn to do things Apple's way in code, but the upside was huge. Meanwhile, the people saying they'll stay with their good old Nokias had to play catch-up eventually...

• Con: You risk putting eggs in someone else's basket. If the company goes under, or decides to quit support in your market, or a myriad of other problems happen, you could be left floundering. And if their programming staff is into featherbedding (taking it easy), you could also have support or updating issues.

• Pro: Time is money. Someone already wrote, debugged, tested and documented the code (at least they had better!) That's time you don't have to spend doing it, and since the cost is likely spread across many customers, that code is cheaper than doing it yourself as a "one-off."

• Con: It's a learning curve. Learning another programmer's code is a job junior programmers have all the time. Senior Programmers thought they'd left most of that behind, until they encounter outside packages; and if they don't want to, they often have the clout to say no to using them.

• Pro: It can expose problems. I once worked with a programmer who didn't want to share. His code was his own, and no one else needed to look at it, or add to it. As far as I know, he's still working for the same company years later, since who else could ramp up on that code? For a programmer hankering for job security, it's a plan that can (unfortunately) work. But for a company that needs to move forward in the market, outside code can help reveal some of the fiefdoms growing in your business, by showing up who resists change the most.

• Con. No fun. We are in this business to program, which is fun for us. Therefore anything that interferes with it interferes with our fun. But programming is a business too, and sometimes it's best to put the fun on hold to get the job done. If a package does that, great.

• Pro: Dipping your toes in the water stretches muscles. Getting used to adapting is good for you. Opens the brain, improves neurons, etc. I once read an example that compared two programmers, one who did the same work each year, repeated year after year for five years, and another who did a new project each year for five years. Guess who was the more well-rounded programmer? So if nothing else, accepting new software challenges (like learning outside codebases) can help you get that roundness going.

Tally up the pros and cons, decide which side you'd prefer to be on, and then do something about it. Remember: NIH doesn't have to afflict you or your loved ones — you CAN take action!

#36: Forget a To-Do List. Plan an "Oh-Oh" List

To-do lists are great — and vital. But also important is an "Oh-oh" list.

Every time I look over a new project I prepare — at least in my head — an Oh-oh list. It's a risk assessment list, keeping track of what can go wrong and what to do if/when it does.

By definition, anything new in the programming realm means new challenges, doing something that wasn't done before. And where there's new there's always a chance something won't work out as planned: That means "oh" (say it with me) "oh." But it's a lot more:

• Programmers love to try new things. New code can be exciting to play with. But it's also hard to plan for and estimate time-wise. What if the code/process/package/component doesn't do everything you want? Do you have a backup? What if the programmer (and that could be you, be honest) didn't understand everything the code could/couldn't do when that shiny new thing was brought on board? You need to plan for unexpected code surprises based on "enthusiastic" expectations.

• Time affects all details. I once worked in house construction. A frame and exterior could be put up in a week; the interior could drag on for a month. Tiny finishing details can be unexpectedly time consuming if you don't plan for them properly.

On one consulting job the manager casually asked me for an estimate, then told me to double it. Turned out, his estimate was a lot closer than mine! Plan for it to take longer than you expect — because it might just.

• What if? What's that old political adage: There are known knowns, known unknowns, and unknown unknowns. It's the unknown unknowns that will get you. You go through a door and naturally expect another room; but if the door opens to the outside and a ten-story drop, that is completely and utterly unexpected (unless you're Wile E. Coyote). In order to plan, you can only — with practice — learn to pad the budget to accommodate the unexpected, which, ironically, you can consistently plan on expecting, even if you can't guess exactly what it is!

• You can have the project done on time, done on budget, or done properly — pick two. That old chestnut sums it up: Eventually you hit the wall and the piper expects to be paid. It's a rare project that is ready on time, so which part will you cut? The right answer is: Anything but quality! Prioritize, keeping some of the less-important features on the back burner, and focus on getting the core code perfected first; in a pinch, you can drop the lesser features. Likewise, it's often possible to get a bit more time by burning the midnight oil, or asking for an extension. However, a program with a few less "side" features is usually preferable to a late project, especially if there is competition.

• Keep backups ready. In manufacturing, they recommend having more than one supplier for everything. Good advice. For programming, it can apply to whatever you might need to replace on short notice. Programmers, equipment, tools and software; really, anything that could stall the project if there was a problem with it. When you have a backup ready for when things get tight, a bad situation doesn't have to get worse.

ALWAYS plan for something failing. Murphy was a smart fellow. Respect him, and his law.

#37: Just Say "No" to Crap Code

Have you ever written crap code?

You haven't? Me neither.

OK, be honest.

That's what I thought. We all have crap code buried somewhere. It's the code you wrote when you were fighting a horrific flu, or when the job needed to be done last month, and the 120-hours-a-week death march began. Or the customer was complaining so much you had to give them something — anything — to stop the barrage. Crap code that, if you'd had time to think it through, would have been much cleaner, much better.

Here's the thing: That bad code will come back to haunt you.

Always.

The core of this book is about getting good habits in place so that good code is written automatically, and bad code "feels" awkward. But it's more than just habits. You also have to get your brain into gear and plan code well, avoiding the temptation to get code out before its time, before it is the best quality. How?

• Develop for goals, not tasks. Counter-intuitively, taking a broader view of problems can make coding easier. For example, are you coding a binary search? No, you're implementing faster access to a sorted list. Viewed that more generalized way, you have many choices: Use a wide variety of pre-sorted lists, hashes, maps, and such to store the data in another fast-access format. Or speed up the access itself by caching previous results, especially useful if each search is close to the previous one (after all, a binary search on a 1,000,000 entry list is slower than a sequential search if the answer is always the first item!) It can pay to step back from the digital trees to see the whole algorithmic forest.

• Get used to your personal rhythms. Sounds new-agey I admit, but for example, if you code great at 2 AM, then try not to put on coding demonstrations at 2 PM. If you write rough code fast but then proofread and polish to a gleam, NEVER let that first draft out of your sight until you've cleaned it up. Know when/where your best code comes from and fight to keep control of it until it's sparkling.

• Never accept "good enough." Ever heard someone say "It's good enough?" They're really saying "I don't want to work on it any longer." Resist that temptation. Let everyone else give up at 70% or 80% or even 90%, but make sure you're the programmer that goes for 100% — or more.

Home staging is the job of setting up a private home to sell. It means putting up pictures on the wall, furnishing every room, even sometimes putting a plate of fresh-baked cookies in the kitchen. None of this is necessary to sell the home; houses are sold all the time without a plate of warm, oozy, double-chocolate chip cookies. But ask a Realtor if it makes a difference in the price, or the speed of selling, or the number of offers. They wouldn't do it if didn't help. Rest assured, for them and for you, doing that extra bit DOES make a difference.

• Learn to think in terms of objects. Eat, sleep, and breathe object-oriented design. I've found over the years it does one thing especially well — you see the boundaries of objects, the fine line between the inside and outside of the object that (as Gandalf says) "you shall not pass." That makes for better code right from the start.

Think of a database: If you view the program as managing the data, then the whole program sticks its grubby fingers into the database whenever it wants, and the code becomes a spaghetti-like mess to maintain and expand.

But think of the database as an object, and now you start thinking differently: It becomes like a walled city, with gates, and everyone goes through those gates. One function does the record update instead of SQL statements scattered through the code, and that one place can now enforce data integrity. A minimal function call list makes coding simpler. And so on. In the end, your code becomes much cleaner and easier to maintain and expand.

• All models are wrong — but some are useful. I think Spock said this (or at least he should have). As soon as someone says "It's like a…" understand two things: 1) It's LIKE it, but not IS it; and 2) For that reason, it may be wrong.

In the previous example, a database is LIKE a bowl of spaghetti, a bad example that leads to bad code. Or it's LIKE a walled city, which helps enforce encapsulation. One is better, but neither are entirely accurate. After all, it's the walls that interest us in the latter; we don't need to carry the city analogy further to include what city hall is, or streets, or the sewage system, for our code to be useful. Take what you need to understand the problem, but remember there is no such thing as a perfect fit, and so don't try too hard to make it fit.

#38: Know When to Break the Rules

Pablo Picasso is known for his weird art. But lest you think it's easier to do because it's weird, do a search on his earlier work. Quite normal — and quite good. Turns out, not just anyone can paint a Picasso; to look that eccentric actually takes quite a bit of skill.

When you get good at coding, you'll develop that same sense. Like a car mechanic who can listen to a car and immediately figure out the problem, you'll just look at code and see where the issues are. You'll also see where you can break the rules as needed.

Take speed. When I first started out, I'd agonize over bytes and cycles, eager to shave time off of every code fragment I wrote (OK, I suppose that urge hasn't gone completely). But now, I know when and where to focus my efforts. For example, over the years, I've realized that GUI interactivity rarely needs optimization, since everything happens at (slow) human speeds. However, GUIs themselves often need

---

major optimization, since refreshes and updates can take tremendous numbers of CPU cycles to "paint" the screen. Therefore: Ignore button-clicking code optimization, but cache and tweak screen repainting. I tend also to cache strings where necessary, since strings are always a speed problem, in every language I've worked in.

So if I've been naughty, and sometimes a GUI's update function is made global, or the string cache is visible outside of a class (but clearly labeled and documented, I'll have you know), it's because I've analyzed the trade-offs in the program and decided the better option — from experience.

The key here is to reserve those tweaks until you really need them. Like optimizing a program, you might only need an adjustment here or there to improve the whole program a great deal. I would in fact argue that if any program needs a lot of tweaking by an experienced programmer, then there's a fundamental issue or two that needs rethinking, like the algorithm or the data format. Most of the time, the code should be ordinary and straightforward. Why? Because experience also tells us that the best code is the code that others can understand, maintain, and improve easily.

There's an old story about a mechanic called in to repair a big machine. He takes a few minutes looking, then taps on one part with a hammer; that fixes things, so he leaves. When the bill arrives, the owner calls and complains about the outrageous price for so little time spent working. The mechanic replies, "1% of the bill is for my time; the other 99% of the bill is for knowing where to hit." Learn your craft well, and you'll end up hitting the right part every time — and hopefully getting properly paid for it as well!

Defensive Programming Is The Only Real Programming

No, it's not programming with an attitude: Like defensive driving, a defensive programmer is on the watch for trouble, to avoid it before it can cause real problems. Everyone else will program the way that they want, so the defensive programmer needs to be on the watch for them — and their mistakes.

#39: Ask Yourself: What If This Fails?

Every line of code does something, so why not get in the habit of asking "What if this line fails?"

Take a simple bit of C code which converts an array of binary ON/OFF values into an ASCII string of 1s and 0s:

```
for (I=0;I<20;++I)
{
  if (0==A[I])
    C[I]='0';
  else if (1==A[I])
    C[I]='1';
}
```

Now you might have some questions:

• What if A has less than 20 elements?

• What if C has less than 20 elements?

• What if C has fewer elements than A?

• Where is the '\0' terminator for C supposed to go?

• Why exactly is I set to 20 anyways?

• And the elephant in the room — what if A[I] is neither 0 nor 1?

By the way, this example is not chosen for practicality (there's easier ways to get a binary string in many languages) but to show how complicated even "simple" code can get. C-style strings just happen to illustrate this point very well!

So to solve this we clamp the loop length to the minimum size of A and C, and decide that all non-zero values of A[I] are set to 1. We'll also stop the array one cell short for C, and put a null byte there:

```
int maxLen=sizeof(A)/sizeof(A[0]); // get A's length
if (maxLen>sizeof(C)/sizeof(C[0]))
  maxLen=sizeof(C)/sizeof(C[0]);    // get C's length
for (I=0;I<maxLen;++I)
{
  if (0==A[I])
    C[I]='0';
  else
    C[I]='1';
}
c[maxLen-1]='\0';
```

Problem solved?

Well, it depends on how general-purpose this code needs to be. For example, what if all of A[] must be converted to a string, regardless of the length of C[]? then you have a problem with design, and if exposed to the big bad world (say, via an Internet interface) a potential for a buffer overrun attack.

Also, this code assumes the arrays are available to the compiler for testing (the sizeof() operators). If we're passing them in as pointers, then a whole bunch of gotchas come up, and the code would likely need rewriting again:

• What if A and/or C are NULL pointers?

• How do we determine length? One way may be to pass in the array size (counts), but then we have questions about invalid values like 0 (which would cause C[maxLen-1] to exception?

Complicated? You bet! But it's this constant "what if" thinking that separates good programmers from those that write code and hope it never fails. "Never" always comes sooner than expected, and by then the code is buried in a long-forgotten part of the program, with the error messages giving no indication of where the problem is (it is my humble opinion that error messages are deliberately designed to mislead programmers).

How to handle code better?

• Play "what if" and learn to anticipate every potential failure of every line.

• When you can anticipate a failure, prevent it if at all possible.

• If you have made any assumptions (like deciding in the sample code that all non-zero values default to 1) then document it for future victims, I mean, programmers.

• If the problems get too big, consider rewriting the code. In our example, changing A[] and I[] from local buffers to pointers brings up so many new issues that the code really would benefit from a complete do-over.

The next tips will go into further details on handling exceptions, but it all starts here with that one habit: At every line of code, ask yourself what could go wrong, and be ready for it.

#40: Assume Nothing in Logic

For many years I've reversed my comparisons between constants and variables: `if(9==K)` instead of `if(K==9)`

The habit developed because my main C compiler at the time would not warn me if I left off one of the equal signs; since you can't assign anything to a constant, this reversal showed up issues right away:

```
if (0=k) // oops!
```

Modern compilers are of course able to catch this, but the habit (which you may or may not want to adopt) highlights a problem with logic: It's, well, logical.

Take the problem I'm seeking to solve — if I accidentally typed this some compilers would only warn (or do even less):

```
if (k=0)
```

After all, in theory I could mean these two statements combined:

```
k=0;
if (k)
```

But how often does this really come up? So a compiler correcting/not correcting this ties its digital hands up, all for the small edge case of a programmer being cute in code.

I know this seems to be nitpicking, but it's to highlight that you can depend on the compiler to catch issues, or you can use tricks so you don't have to, and therefore still safely work with a twonky compiler.

For example:

• As mentioned, reversing constants and variables in a test catches some errors and is easy to do. If you work in different languages, a habit like this can make a real difference. For example, switching between BASIC and C, it's easy to leave off the second equals in a C test, which is not used in BASIC.

• Edge conditions can cause real problems with equals/not equals. If you're working with libraries like the STL you may have no choice (iterators work on equal/not equal for boundary testing) but elsewhere, you can try to use a range test: `< <= >= >` instead of `== !=`. The benefit here is if for some reason code skips over the edge condition, you'll catch it. This happens far more often than you might expect, especially if a quick change adjusts the loop's end. For example, a careless edit changes this

```
for (k=0;k!=10;k+=2)
```

to this

```
for (k=1;k!=10;k+=2)
```

And voila — instant infinite loop! In contrast, `k<10` would have prevented the error.

One caution with edge conditions around zero. If your variables are unsigned, they can never go negative, so this is one case where the equals/not equals test is a good idea.

• Go crazy with the parenthesis. Tests should be obvious, and so if a complicated test takes a few moments for the next programmer to puzzle out, why not make it easier and turn

```
if ( ++K <= ++M )
```

into

```
if ( (++K) <= (++M) )
```

Better yet, leave off the side effects — these days, C is plenty fast without jamming everything onto the same line:

```
++K;
++M;
if ( K <= M )
```

• Balance practical and cautious. You can add a ton of tests in code. For example, if you are working with files, you can check every step, from opening to reading to closing, or you can use a try/catch to handle most of the exceptions. Checking for division by zero, or if there is a memory under-run are common issues that can explode the number of lines for error checking. Yes, memory runs out, and sometimes zeroes are divided unfairly; but if you add thirty tests in a small function of ten lines, it might be time to analyze the code, and ask yourself why the data is not in better shape by the time it gets there!

#41: Floating Point Is a World Unto Itself

I think the human brain has issues with floating point.

Defensive Programming Is The Only Real Programming

Well actually it's computers that do; we just have a problem understanding their CPU-based stupidity.

Take 0.1, a perfectly valid floating point number. We know it's exactly one tenth, no more and no less. But a computer can't represent it exactly in floating point, and we need to help it. So how?

• Understand where we and computers agree/disagree. 0.1 might make us think we're smarter than a computer, but we're just using a different data representation, one convenient for us (base 10). For example, when we write 1/3, we're saying we want an exact value that we can't write as a decimal fraction (0.3333…) much like a computer saying it can't store 0.1 using powers of two. In contrast, 0.5, 0.25, 0.125 and so on fall in its "sweet spot", just like 0.1 for us. But in the end, we all have limits in how we represent certain numbers — just different numbers (although we can all agree that irrational numbers are a pain.)

• If you have to use comparisons, avoid equals. Since floating point results can be quite close yet still not exact (for example, 1.0!=1.00000000001), better to use a range than try for equality. If you need to be equal to 1.0 for example, ask yourself if this safer version will work:

```
if ( 0.99<X && X<1.01 )
```

• Learn to clamp. Your IDE may say a value is 1.0, but the number may really be 1.0000000001 internally, so get in the habit of clamping values whenever necessary. It may not seem important, but even a slight overflow can cause rare (and therefore hard-to-debug) problems. I encountered this once when doing graphical calculations on RGB colors. Without clamping to a maximum of 255, every once in a while a value would go over 255 and "infect" the next byte in my 3-byte RGB value, messing with the colors.

Most languages have a min() and max() function, so this should work fine:

```
X=Math.Min(X,255.0)
X=Math.Max(0.0,X)
```

Even better, clamp high and low at the same time like this:

```
X=Math.Max(0.0,Math.Min(X,255.0))
```

Two cautions: There are many ways of clamping values. Some round up (often called ceiling), some round down (floor or truncate), some do either depending on the value (round). Pick appropriately. Also, if the number range can be above and below an integer value (like 0.9999999 to 1.0000001) understand that truncating this could end up with either 0 or 1 for a valid result, clearly not what you want. In this case, add a small offset before clamping to make sure the proper value is always there:

```
int X=(int)(X+0.1)
```

• Understand the limits of your floating point. The exponent can cover a huge range, but a calculation can still go too far. The IEEE 754 specification defines a single precision floating point as 32 bits long, or from about 10^{-38} to 10^{+38}, so if you need a larger (or smaller) number, you'll need a 64-bit Double, which has a range of about 10^{-308} to 10^{+308}.

• Scaling is a problem to watch out for. If you add 0.000000000000000000001 to 1,000,000,000,000,000,000 and get the same 1,000,000,000,000,000,000 then you're a victim of too wide a calculation range. Moving to a larger precision will work, but if you aren't prepared for the result, it can look like the math is wrong, when in fact it's just "shifted-out" by extreme values.

• Speed is always a consideration. I started programming with floating point when it was done with multiple instructions, and no Floating Point Unit (FPU). Back then, FP could really slow down a computer doing calculations, so there were all sorts of tricks to avoid it. Now with a floating point coprocessor it's not an issue, but still worth being aware of. Why? Because not all computers have a FPU. For example the Arduino slowly multiplies with shift+addition code loops, and division is far slower than multiplication. But even if you don't plan to work with the Arduino, there are other devices that lack a FPU (Internet Of Things, anyone?), so it will remain relevant.

• The past's optimization tricks are rarely necessary today. I originally wanted to add tips here on how to avoid floating point, such as strength reduction (for example changing 2*X into X+X to avoid a multiply) or breaking them into integer or bit shift operations (such as 0.25*X converted into X>>4) but nowadays compilers are very good at analyzing code and adding in their own optimizations. As well, there's often problems with optimization: They work until the code gets tweaked (like 0.25*X changed to 0.1*X, which is not so simple to bit shift), and they can be pretty awkward to understand, and therefore harder to document; all of which makes it easier to get it wrong.

The moral of the story? Floating point should always give you pause. Use it, but understand it's not like a precise int or long; it's a scruffy, partially opaque number format that might not always be exactly as it appears…

#42: The Simple Stuff'll Getyuh

As I've mentioned many, many (many) times in this guide, habits are handy, a way to speed up the grunt work. The brain tries to put information into patterns it can repeat again and again — habits — because it likes to go on automatic pilot as much as possible (that's the highly advanced scientific explanation). So here's another batch of coding "gotchas" that are worth practicing again and again until they are habitual, thus saving your massive brain power for the real coding:

• Boundary conditions. Boundary (or edge) conditions are where all the action happens. Loop from 0 to 99, and loop values 1 through 98 are pretty much the same (barring conditionals in the code of course). But loop 0 is where the code enters the loop, and initialization conditions are set up (and possibly set up wrong). Likewise, the last loop is where things leave, and whatever the loop was doing to values, stops.

In my experience, debugging loops always involves most of the effort at the start and the end, making sure what goes in and what comes out is correct. If I walk through a couple of loops at the start and end in the debugger, and a couple for the "middle" values, I feel quite confident the code will run fine for all looping. If you walk through your code with the debugger (and you should), remember to pay special attention to those boundaries.

• Off by one. This is another issue like boundary conditions, and appears everywhere. Errors happen easily — how often have you changed a loop, say from `(Y=0;Y<7;++Y)` to `(Y=1;Y<=7;++Y)`? It still loops the same number of times, but now all indexes are off by one, and more than likely need `[Y-1]` changes where they used to be `[Y]`. Add to that different indexing issues with different languages (where for example it's easy for BASIC programmers to forget that the last index in C for `X[15]` is 14, not 15), and you risk errors creeping in.

• Pre/post conditions. Does it matter whether you use `++N` or `N++`? With a good optimizing compiler, not likely, but if yours isn't then it makes a teeny, tiny bit of optimization benefit (and is significant if you create a C++ class with post- and pre- increment) The issue? `++N` can increment and return the incremented value immediately, whereas `N++` has to increment and then return the old value, requiring it to store that value briefly, thus using a bit of extra storage and time.

But more importantly, these conditions matter if you combine them in calculations or tests. For example, are you comfortable when you encounter a C test like this?

```
If (i++<6)
```

Going in, is i=5 true or false? What about 6? Or 4? Practicing this type of analysis until it's second nature will give you coding speed.

• Buffers. Arguably, one of the worst problems on the Internet for security today is buffer overruns. Put a baker's dozen of doughnuts into a box sized for twelve and it stretches and possibly splits: But write 1,000,000 bytes to a buffer sized to hold 128, and really bad things happen.

You should never go beyond your buffer — ever. That includes both front and back. In C/C++ it's perfectly allowable to address outside of the buffer, although many other languages have built-in checks. This is where off by one errors are especially annoying, because one byte before the start of an array or one byte after may do very little, or it may do a lot. Imagine a C/C++ buffer on the stack created as part of a function, and when the function returns, a buffer overrun has corrupted the last byte of the caller stack. Depending on the architecture of the CPU, and the compiler, maybe the byte was extra space (for example, because a variable was padded to align in the computer's memory properly). Or maybe it was part of the return address, and the function doesn't return properly. And so on. Moral of the story? If your language does not manage memory, make sure you take care. At the very least, use safe calls for copies, moves and such in memory, like `strcpy_s()` instead of `strcpy()` in C++.

• Always initialize. I'm going to break this rule immediately by saying there are exceptions to "always": If you had to initialize every buffer with every function call, some programs would grind to a halt. But let those exceptions be few and far between. For many languages, you don't even have to worry, since variables are initialized at creation. But for others, it can be a pain to do so, yet is a very, very important habit to get into. The main example of naughtiness is C/C++, where uninitialized variables can contain any leftover garbage. If you program in that language, take a look at any function you code, and ask yourself what would happen if random values accidentally got into the code. Get in the practice of initializing whenever possible, and don't be afraid to carry it over to other languages — I often set my variables to 0 in Java and BASIC even though I know I don't have to. There is a certain comfort in visually asserting what they should be.

• Clean up after yourself. Set up your arrays and buffers nicely, and get rid of them nicely. In the languages where you manage memory yourself, delete them and NEVER USE THEM AGAIN. I routinely set C pointers to NULL as soon as I free memory — even if it's the last line in a function and the pointer is local. It's a habit that prevents the pointer being accidentally reused, which has happened on occasion (particularly with longer functions where the memory was freed many lines earlier).

If the language manages the memory via garbage collection, there's no problem of writing to bad memory if you do reuse the object, but you may risk creating multiple references to a memory chunk, and thereby preventing garbage collection from clearing it away. In that case, if the object is truly done, I'm in the habit of setting it to `nothing` or `null` or whatever that language requires, to let it get cleaned up as soon as possible.

• Avoid the sugar. Syntactic sugar is a fancy term for code that's pretty, but isn't absolutely necessary for the program to run. You see this often in classes: Take for instance overloading the array operator in C++. With it, you can do something exotic like

```
x["d:\\file.ext"]="some string";
```
And have it save a string to the file. Bizarre, but possible. It's not really necessary, so why not just use a regular function to save a string to a file, and make the code easier to understand as well?

Now there is a balance needed here, since overloading can make some code simpler to understand. But writing oddball code just to play with features is not a good idea in production code, as it makes everything harder to read, harder to maintain, and harder to port (and a fair bit of code ends up ported). Plus confusing: Code like this example would generally look like a dictionary entry changed or created, keyed to the string `"d:\\file.ext"`. So the next programmer not only needs to understand your new mini-language and syntax, but also what the code is meant to do — an unnecessary maintenance double-whammy. But syntactic sugar, like beauty, is in the eye of the beholder, so use it if you wish. However, as a rule of thumb, if the language has to be massaged a lot to do what you want it to do, consider just making it a straightforward function call.

#43: Cast Yea No More!

Casting has a bad rap. I personally hate it, since every cast draws a line in the sand about a variable. If I cast an `int` to a `double`, and a week later decide `single` will do, I have to wander through my code making changes. So much of good coding involves self-contained code, variables and classes that hide information. Add a cast and you add a public bit of info at each spot. So casting feels like someone didn't do the right job at the beginning in picking the variable type. If you remember Hungarian notation (where the variable name including a letter code for the type, like "i" in front for integer), then you've encountered this awkward branding before.

But I do understand there are times:

• For example, perhaps you're doing some coding between languages or OS layers, talking to a third-party interface, or you're reading and writing bytes in a specified order. There, casts might be needed to enforce the interface. But try to place them in a single location and avoid casts elsewhere. For example, wrap that function call in another thin function call that manages the casts, so you can pass the variables to the outer call without massaging. And if you have a lot of casts, consider changing the variable type itself to reduce them.

• If you do need to cast, make them large and obvious. Make them take up a whole line by themselves, include a large comment, and generally make them stand out and be ugly, so ugly that everyone who comes by it in the code says "yikes." Hopefully, the author of the code you're interfacing with also comes by, takes a look at the code you're force to cast to, and is embarrassed into rewriting it so they aren't necessary.

• Oh, and take everything I just said and ignore it in the case of `const`. NEVER, NEVER, cast away `const`! If a value should never be changed, telling the compiler "it's OK" does not make it OK. You might get away with it occasionally (say a `const` class that is actually mutable in C++), but quite often you won't, and when it blows, it blows up bad.

Bottom line: Casts are annoying, and you should avoid them if at all possible.

#44: Two (Computer) Minds Are Better Than One

Your finely-crafted program is done, a thing of beauty. Confidently, you feed it some real-world data, and it fails.

Sound familiar?

Programming, to me, is often less about initial problem solving, and more about fine tuning after the fact. No matter how much we anticipate, there always seems to be an exception, and sometimes it can be very a big one.

Take for instance the Therac-25. In the 1980s it was a medical machine that sent a dose of radiation in order to cure. Now of course, no one wants too much radiation, and this device had safeguards to prevent that. Unless you fiddled with the settings too much. Like one of those video game cheat codes, if you did this and that and then this, it unlocked high power. Great for a video game, lethal for users of this machine.

If I sound flippant, I'm not. People died over this software error.

Think of that: People Died From A Software Bug.

Before the problem was caught and fixed, six people received too much radiation, and three died (and by the way, Wikipedia uses the term "documented cases" for these six — who really knows how much undocumented suffering went on?)

So, you have a program that can kill people. What do you do?

Safeguards. Lots of safeguards.

For example, once this program was ready to send a dose, a second routine could run. That routine's job is to note the dosage, and scream out an alert if it's above a specific level. Simple (in hindsight). Ironically, previous versions of the device had hardware safeguards that worked very well; they removed them since they felt the software could handle it.

In the real world, we ask someone to check over our results. In the computer world this works, too:

• If you do a calculation, consider a redundant calculation to check it, using a different formula, for example.

Defensive Programming Is The Only Real Programming

• Writing a file? Another program or routine could read it in and verify it. More often than not, the file will be read in by your software anyway, so why not have the writing and reading routines do a cross check of each other's results?

• Create routines to have the program verify data itself whenever possible. Called invariants, they check to make sure everything is, well, invariant (not varying outside of valid parameters). For example, in one program I needed to make sure the database was safe after each change, so I wrote an invariant function to verify that every object in one table was referenced properly in another, items were sequentially numbered, there were no duplicate id numbers, and so on. This was valuable on those occasions when new code broke something, as non-sequential or unlinked object records showed up right away, before they could cause serious problems in the production code.

• One easy way to perform this extra checking is with assertions, which are one-line invariants. Often in the form of

```
assert(statement that's normally true,"displayed message if not")
```

These statements allow you to check that things are correct in debug mode, and warn you of issues. For some cases they are ideal (for example, making sure you're using a function correctly, or blowing up if you pass an empty array when a full one is expected). However, they can only enforce the internal consistency inside the program, checking that the programmer's code is not failing — you can't use these to check outside data (like user input) since they disappear in production code, removed when debug mode is turned off.

• A more vigorous way of computerized double-checking is a whole philosophy, test driven development (TDD). With TDD you write a test for a small portion of the problem, get that test to fail (thereby testing the test), then write code that passes the test. Repeat this, adding new code until the program is done. There's frequent code cleanup involved too, but you get the general idea. Over time, you create a body of test code that goes along with the working code, so you not only test the code as you write it, but also as you rewrite/maintain it (since changes will have to pass the tests as well). The advantage is that, unlike assertions, you can test with production data, since this code can remain active even when debug mode is turned off.

Whenever possible, use the computer to test and check. After all, if the data is too important to leave unchecked, then check it — it's that simple.

#45: Don't Be a Hog

Some programs (and programmers) like resources a lot. But whenever you can, use the minimum:

• Memory. If you can do the work in less memory, why not? I once worked on an algorithm for a maze in a game. On a small device (the Palm Pilot) the code crashed, because the recursive routine to generate the maze took up too much stack space. Changing recursion into a loop got rid of the stack usage, and the program ran fine.

• Oftentimes, it's possible to read a file, get the data you need, and then close the file, rather than keeping it open during processing, and hogging that I/O resource. Here you're trading one resource (disk files) for another (memory) but if you're going to hog something, memory usually has less impact on a system than file I/O. Unless it's a really large amount of memory: Then you're stuck, since on modern systems it ends up being paged to disk anyways, and now you've replaced your file's I/O with "hidden" page file I/O.

• Time hog? Well-designed data elements and better algorithms can speed up a program. Frequently I've found that improving how the data format interacts with the algorithm improves performance everywhere. Take for example reading in a Yes/No array; a simple program might write out each value as an ASCII character `0/1` (or worse yet the actual words `true`/`false` — don't laugh, Visual BASIC does). Decoding that file involves a fair bit of code, extra memory, and slower performance than necessary. Code it as a binary file however (where each on/off value is a byte or even a bit in the array), and the data is smaller, faster, and just about ready to use as soon as you read it in.

• Obviously, balance is needed. You can save time by using more memory; you can save memory by packing data or calculating values on the fly instead of caching them; and so on. Each has their pros and cons. In the end, be aware of the issue, and be ready to attack the worst hog in the bunch. Once that one is conquered, you may find that the performance becomes "good enough" and no more tweaks are needed to get the job done.

Practice reducing resource usage whenever possible: It will stand you in good stead in the future when you hit a real crunch, like a program that is so big and sluggish that you'll need to trim every ounce of algorithmic fat off of it to get it to work.

#46: Trust No One

In a nutshell, this means to verify all data that you do not have complete control over:

• Obviously, user data is always suspect. Users have a near-infinite capacity to misunderstand what you think is crystal clear. Try and anticipate issues, and verify or otherwise tidy up everything that comes in.

• Program settings are suspect. INI files used to be a common way of saving program settings. Because they were a text file, many people got in the habit of editing them manually with a text editor, and possibly (likely) screwing up the values.

Registry data, database files — someone can and will tweak them someday, so it pays to verify even those things.

• It's not just data in, it's the environment. For example, I had a program that saved its window position before quitting. One time I changed to a smaller monitor resolution, and the window disappeared when run, because the old position was now off the viewscreen's edges. A sanity check of the data against the current window size would have caught the problem (and eventually did, once I coded it!)

• And let's not forget HTML data. Local forms might have data errors that are troublesome, but on the web, those errors may also be malicious. Not only can you not trust the data from a web form, you can expect someone, someday, will deliberately try to break something using bad input data. Get militant about verifying user data from the web.

• That it? No. You also can't trust the operating system. When you ask for something, don't expect a big "Hello" and a firm handshake; expect a whiny baby. Operating systems have a contract of sorts with programs: Ask for what you need, and they will provide it if possible. At least until it's not possible. Then it just ignores you, kills your program, blames you for the issue (or at least tech support will when you talk to them) and more. Add to that the interactions from all the pieces attached to the OS (virus programs, for example) and you know you're on your own with any issues. Ask the operating system for what you need, but ask yourself at the same time just what can go bad — and anticipate it.

Not all data checking needs to be intensive. Just confirming a value is one of several valid values, or that the values are set, may be enough. Even a simple check-sum can make a world of difference for protecting some kinds of data, or a "Validate database" menu option in your program. The alternative is the chance of bad inputs screwing up your program, whether deliberately or accidentally.

The data coming in must be clean if you have any hope of your code doing what it is meant to do. If you've ever heard the phrase "Garbage In, Garbage Out" this is where it came from — bad data in means bad results out.

#47: Invariably, Invariants Are Your Friend

I first heard of the topic of invariants when studying Eiffel, one of the earlier object-oriented programming languages. An invariant was a way to enforce the contract between the function and the caller: Simply put, it showed up errors fast.

Languages like C and JavaScript can bury their errors. If things go wrong, they just don't work (until they blow up of course). This is handy in a production situation, where failure to work is better than a major meltdown (but only marginally!)

However, if you're debugging the code, you face a real problem when an error is hidden. There, you need to know what's wrong, ideally as soon as it happens, so burying an error and letting it propagate (and often grow) is counterproductive.

An invariant changes all that: It's code that you use to guarantee the function is working according to specification. Take a contrived example, where you write a specialty square root function (maybe not too contrived — I actually did one of these, using Newton's algorithm, for a micro-controller w/o a floating point unit).

Now we all know it's taboo to take the square root of a negative number, but how should we handle this "issue" in the function:

- Exit and do nothing, passing back whatever partial/invalid result it may have.

- Return with a dummy value, say -1.

- Exception out.

- Scream blue murder and shut down everything.

The problem is simple: The function, as it stands, fails on negative numbers; if the program calls it with a negative number, it too will fail. No amount of sugarcoating (either to your manager, or syntactic sugarcoating) will fix that. So what is best?

In this case, the program needs a "contract" with the function: I promise to not send you negatives, and you promise to give me a valid square root. The program code then checks for valid inputs before calling the function. Likewise, the function enforces its "terms" with appropriate checks. This is reasonable because no one should ask for a negative's square root here. More importantly, it is beyond the function's ability to provide it, so blowing up right away is better than fudging the return and passing on the problem down the line.

That's where the invariant comes in. At the beginning of the function is a simple test:

```
assert(inVal>=0,"invalid negative number passed to sqrt()");
```

Any **assert()** in code (which is meant to be active in debug code only) tests the first term; if an error occurs — in this case if **inVal>=0** is false — then the program grinds to a halt. However, that's the nuclear option for what may be a small bug, and unfortunately, (mixed metaphors a'coming) if you're always walking on eggshells you end up tiptoeing, when sometimes you really need to break a few eggs.

Many years ago I read about an assertion that was more generic and gentle. When it failed, it gave 3 options, Abort, Retry, and Ignore:

- Abort is similar to the good old **assert()** — the program stops. But instead of ending it all, it breaks into the debugger near the error, so I can examine it. After all, if it's only active in a debug version of the program, why not use the debugger? And since I'm in the debugger, I can resume the program after, something the older assert function couldn't do.

• Retry. In this case, no breaking, and the code continues on. However, if this assertion is ever hit again, and fails again, I'll get this message again.

• Ignore. Like Retry, processing continues, but this time the assert is "turned off" so it is bypassed from now on, never to be called again (in this run, that is.)

I liked it so much I wrote a variation, called ASSERTING(), and used it in my code. Over the years, I've also seen this 3-way assert variation appear in some languages, and I've also ported it to just about every system I worked on because it's so darn useful:

• Some errors are easy to skip. For example, if there's one error in a loop, then I can expect the loop will blow up with each pass. So turn it off and continue the test run. Say I have a page number issue (my report starts with page 0). I make a note of the error, but do I need to stop the whole program for that? No, so I select the Ignore option and I won't be bothered with it for the rest of the run. Easy peasy.

• With less "pain" on each failure (no automatic program exiting), there's no penalty for checking, so I am inclined to add more checks. This lets me catch more errors as they happen, and most importantly, while I'm still debugging.

• Even a fatal error should be investigated, not given up on. Frankly, I never understood why the old assert existed. I can write a function myself that blows up the program (many times in fact, and sadly without even meaning to), so why enshrine it in debug code? But an assert that breaks to the code in the IDE is extremely valuable. From there, I can check the variables, the stack, and more.

• Abort lets me go to the code AND go back to running. In that way, it's like retry with a pit stop to investigate first. In some IDEs, it even lets me change variables and "patch" an error while running, so I don't have to restart the program after each and every major problem.

Although I've found this routine invaluable through the years (as I say, I've ported it to just about every OS and compiler I've worked on) it does have one issue: Since it needs a dialog to interact with the programmer, it's not useful for GUI-less code, such as embedded code, or code for real-time processing (where you can't pause any user interface). In cases like that, you'll probably have to endure the old fashioned **assert()** function, or log errors. But for most every other case, find it in your IDE and use it: It makes a huge difference in debugging your software!

#48: On Being Appropriately Testy

Obviously, I like assertions. I also like test harnesses, and testing regimens like TDD (although I admit I don't always follow them). Throwing exceptions are an option as well. But there are only so many hours in the day to write test code, and managers generally want you to do production code once in a while. So how to balance things?

• Obviously, you can't test everything. Take the square root example. In theory, to test the code completely requires sending it every single number in existence. And if you think that is needlessly wasteful (!), look up the Pentium FDIV bug, where approximately one in a billion floating point divides would be wrong — imagine the test bed to catch that bug! Nonetheless, an example like that should make you humble about testing, not be an excuse to ignore testing entirely.

• Generally, I test edge conditions, assumptions, and (like the square root of -1) expected issues. For example, a reasonably thorough square root test would include checks for very large values, very small, and obvious items like -1, 0, and +1 (assumptions, remember?) Edge conditions would include numbers like -0.0000001 and +0.0000001, to make sure "nearby" values are OK, too. Possibly as you read this you're thinking up similar test entries. One advantage of TDD is that you think carefully of the tests before writing the code, which I believe exerts a subtle pressure to explore the problem in greater detail.

• Assert versus test bed versus throwing exceptions? I like them all, for different reasons. Very roughly speaking, I like assertions for things that should never change within the code, throwing for things users might want to be aware of (and control) and test beds to catch data oddities and exceptions, like edge cases and unusual values.

Take for instance (again) the square root function: I would add an assert for the minimum and maximum numbers I process in my function. This is my contract with the user, in this case, the programmer calling my function; give me only valid numbers and I will give you a valid result. If I felt there was a chance of misuse in production code, or I felt the user needed more control, I would also add exception throwing. Finally, I would create a test function that would check every edge condition I could think of, and throw good and bad values at it, to make sure I get the results I expect, and to alert me if future changes break current code. (Note that the test cases and the asserts won't play nicely together, since assertions want to exit the program flow if an error is found, so I'd have to turn off the assertions during my testing run.)

• Be wary of throwing. I general avoid throwing exceptions. One reason as I mentioned earlier is the time penalty they can add. The main reason however is that it adds a maintenance burden to the programmer using my function, one I'm not always happy with. After all, should the user of my square root function now have to catch custom exceptions like

EXCEPTION_NUMBER_TOO_LARGE
EXCEPTION_NUMBER_TOO_SMALL

And anything else I add just because I think they might need it? Forcing programmers to handle every exception is a big bugaboo in Java, one I find annoying. For small functions like this, I would prefer to use assertions to catch interface errors. The programmer can then add an exception to the test if they want to; for example, by creating a wrapper function around this one that performs the same tests as my assertions do, but throwing errors for each. Nonetheless, throwing exceptions makes for cleaner code, so I will use them, just not any- and every- where.

• Consider a test-first philosophy. It's more work to write tests, then write code, then repeat. You write more code overall, and think about the problem from both sides (how it can work, and how it can break). But these become assets, since over time you start thinking of code in terms of "so how can I prove that code works," which influences your coding style.

For example, recently one function I was working on ended up being an almost exact duplicate of another, just with different data passed in. In the past I would have written them both, kept them close together in the source code, and placed numerous comments about how they must stay in sync. But thinking of it in terms of testing, I created a single function, and I passed in a function pointer for a data reading routine. In one case, the function feeds in real data; in another, test data. The same function now can work on two data "kinds" that will always be in sync, instead of two functions processing two copies of data, and hoping maintenance keeps them working identically forever and ever.

• Invest in your tests. Keep them clean and tidy, and up to date. Run them often. If one fails, dig into why; don't just turn it off. And as problems arise, add those new bugs to the test bed to verify the fixes.

• Tests are forever. Understand they are not just there to make your coding correct as you write it the first time. They'll also catch future errors as you change code. When you add features, the tests passing or failing will alert you if your new code is correct or not. The more tests, the more confidence you can have in changes. The result? Much easier maintenance.

Understand your code's use and test appropriately. It will pay now, and in the future. Guaranteed.

A GUI Is Worth 1,024 Words

In the beginning, it was command lines and text. But for many, many years, appearances have mattered, and the Graphical User Interface is now the face of almost every program out there. GUIs are important for ease of use, and make the client happy; so for their sake at least, it pays to understand graphical interfaces well.

#49: GUI Design is ALWAYS a Compromise

The goal of GUI design is to make the user understand what to do, and to make it easy to do something.

And we always fail. So get used to it.

Years ago, I watched my Dad use a mouse for the first time. Went great, proving that the mouse is perhaps the best user interface device ever invented.

Did I say "great?" No, I meant it went horribly. The mouse pointer was jittery and moved too fast for him, and he found actually resting his hand on the mouse was a very awkward action — and moving it around while in that position was equally awkward.

Hard to believe? Switch the mouse right now from your dominant hand to the other, and the do some game playing, or visit a few pages on the Internet.

We get used to the horrible interfaces we've been given. Don't get me wrong, the mouse is very, very useful, but it's clunky for newbies (I frankly wonder when someone is going to launch a multi-million dollar class action lawsuit for mice causing Carpal Tunnel syndrome). However, my point here is not just the mouse, but interfaces in general. They suck. They all do. Our job as designers is to reduce the sukkage factor.

Think I'm extreme? Look at a button on the computer screen — any button.

Surprise! It's not a button. It's a collection of pixels that looks vaguely button-like. Sometimes not even vaguely, since lately the trend has been away from realistic 3D items and more "flat."

So if you were a computer newbie using a particular program, you'd first need to learn the whole press-a-button-to-do-something way of working, then learn the kinda-sorta computer version of a button, then finally how to use it like a real button (how to "click").

And if that's not enough, once you've related it to the real world, everything falls apart: After all, how many real-world buttons have you worked with actually change colors, labels, shape or size when you click on it? Or disappear?

Now I'm not saying we have to rethink user interface design (I am, but here is not the place to discuss it); what I am saying is that if we can view the GUI with a newbie's eyes, we'll realize that a close connection between the real world and our visual ideas is vital for easy learning — and the further we separate the two the harder it is for people to learn. It can never be perfect, since we'd be foolish not to use some of the novel options computers provide for feedback, After all, a button that changes color IS a handy alert.

But the goal of interface design is to map the computer design model onto the user's current worldview as close as reasonably possible. We can't do it exactly, but remembering that should at least help us be humble as we design interfaces.

#50: Users Really Don't Care

Our software is great.

It is. It really is.

News flash: We might be the only ones who believe that.

Our users don't. They are here to get a job done. Maybe it's a report, a spreadsheet, or a video conference call. But the design is second to the job.

Don't believe me? Can you describe the view screen of your favorite game in detail? I can't. Sure, run it and I can find my way around no problem. But where exactly is the health display, the score, and the inventory on the screen? I can't even tell you what my current game avatar is wearing, and I went to a lot of effort to "dress" him! Plus remember we spend hours on video games. In contrast, many users want to get a task done in minutes with an unfamiliar program and then forget about it.

The point is, no matter how much care we put into designing things, we need to remember our clients will probably never "feel it" like we do.

Why does this matter?

• Too many times, the desire to stand out, rather than help the client, forces adoption of designs that are bad. I think someone should be taken to task for all those flat GUI designs out there now. They are actually harder for new users to adapt to versus 3D or photo-realistic interfaces. But one company did it, so everyone has to play catch-up. If we really cared about what the client wants, usability studies would have stopped the whole "flat" movement right at the start.

• Interesting effects and add-ons frequently get in the way of a user and his/her job. "Chrome" can refer to the unnecessary glitz applied to a program. The number of times I've seen colors schemes, effects, and animation that helped me understand a program is practically zero (I'm talking to you, Clippy!) If it's not vital to the program, I would argue that it actually interferes with using it. Different means new, and few people really want to learn new for its sake alone. Make everyone's life easier, and add effects that enhance — and only those effects.

• We are too close, and need to step back a bit. Like the example of my Dad and the mouse, we programmers/power users have learned things we need to unlearn if we want users to literally "get with the program." We're immersed in them, completely familiar with them; so that desire for change, for something new and different is strong, but only for us. Everyone else will be OK with the same-old-same-old (except the Marketing Department of course). Frankly, if I had an operating system user interface that didn't change every few years, I'd prefer it. And I know I'm not alone in this.

You may have an uphill battle in your company to keep things from changing frequently, but just remember that users don't care about new nearly as much as you do.

#51: Annoyed User = Former User

Your goal is to get your client in and working with your product ASAP. Any "odd" ways of doing so steepen the learning curve, and risk them giving up. After all, users do have other things to do besides using your program.

What are some problem areas?

• Modes. A button does this in this mode, then does that in another. Modes are unnatural in the real world, and they require some brain power to get used to. For example, on a computer users have to be familiar with control keys, and how the regular keys change their meaning if you hold Alt or Ctrl or that other key down first. Even something as simple as the Caps Lock button is confounding. On an old-fashioned typewriter (is that an oxymoron yet?) that key physically elevated the other keys, gave a nice "clunk" sound, and stayed down, all feedback to let you know things were going to be different now. But on a computer keyboard, a key that stays down costs extra to build, so it just toggles; and while you're typing suddenly your finger slips AND ALL THE WORDS YOU TYPE ARE IN CAPITALS. Modes are annoying: Remove them if possible, explain them if not, but reduce them as much as you can.

• Different (digital) strokes for different folks — and tasks. A mouse is better for random or unanticipated positioning and selection, while a keyboard is better/faster for anticipated ones. That's why keyboard shortcuts are still around, and we use them a lot in word processors and text editors — our hands are already at the keyboard, so a key command is close by and straightforward. But if you've ever tried to move a graphic program's items around with the arrow key, you understand the power of the mouse for those quick and/or somewhat-random movements. Use the tool that suits the task.

• If the option is common, the way to select it should be common. When DOS first came out, Ctrl+Alt+Del would restart the computer — combining three keys to do something rarely wanted and very, very dangerous to perform made sense. Likewise, a simple option (like capitalizing a word) should be simple, and it is: Hold down the Shift key as you type. Or use the Caps Lock — but remember to turn it off after!

• Change is bad. Menus are a great example of this. Some programs hide advanced options and provide a "beginner" menu, expecting you to turn on the more advanced options when you need them. What they don't seem to realize is that learning two menus is NOT easier. And it is two: The beginner's menu and then the advanced one they'll need eventually. Yes, a huge selection of menu options can be overwhelming to look at, but that's why submenus exist — at least the position remains the same, and oddball settings can stay hidden until finally needed. Rearranging objects and display elements once you've finally memorized their locations just makes the learning harder.

• Software needs to be polite and helpful. Which is easier to program: "Your file is corrupted" or "Unable to save your file due to lack of disk space. Please select another location to save." Trick question, since they both require roughly the same effort. One of them scares the user with a problem but leaves out the cause, or any solution; the other specifies the problem the user has and offers a solution. Taking a little extra effort to avoid annoying users is good for programmers to understand, and it's good business as well.

• Give users the explanation in a way they can understand. In the previous "good" error message, the client understands the problem is in the computer (no hard drive space) and gives them a reasonable option so as to bypass it (pick a new location). In the bad error message, there are few details. Now think of it: You're trying to "save" something and you can't. If you're saving money, it's in a bank account. If you're saving baseball cards, they are in a box under your bed. But saving a file means it is currently — where? Programmers understand the file system fine, but the typical user has little real-world experience that can relate to something like a hard drive (and no, file cabinets don't count, unless your average client uses one constantly). So how are they supposed to react if you don't explain things in a way they can understand?

• Don't zone out without warning. Handheld devices are really bad for this. If a program goes slow or pauses, I want to know it's busy and not crashed. An active progress bar/spinner display is something we're used to and willing to wait for (somewhat). But just stopping the screen for a few seconds is bad, bad, bad.

There is a story that Steve Jobs made sure the cursor on the original Macintosh ran independently, so that the display would always appear responsive. Sadly, with his iOS devices that care is gone, and programs hang, typically with no alert whatsoever. And not just iOS — I never know whether to reboot or wait on my Android tablet. Often, I give up and get myself to the nearest desktop. Keep the client informed on delays, because if the program freezes, they won't blame the OS; they'll blame your program.

#52: Understand the Battle Between Veterans and Newbies

As I've already mentioned, newbies have different ideas about how software should work. With effort, we get used to the ways that things are done, and become veterans. And at that point we often forget what it was like to try and fail in a typical GUI. But as designers it's important to remember our roots.

For example, Windows is not really full of windows. It's tiled areas onscreen of semi-private data. There's no peeking though into a new world, like outside of our house or car (except perhaps for video games). It would have been more accurately called "Bulletin Board", or "Note Cards On A Wall."

But the analogy is kinda-sorta close, so we accept it. A window "seems" to contain its visual elements, and we are familiar with windows having something inside them that doesn't get "outside" (glass, a view, etc). So that thing we understand helps us learn something new. But a newbie hears "windows" and expects a bit different.

That's not the only disconnect between a beginner's hard-won real world knowledge and our computer representation of things:

• A click should do something. There's a clicking sound for a reason! When we press a button — once — in the real world, we expect something to happen. Not necessarily on the computer, since we also have the double-click, where the first click is ignored. Do you know anyone who double-clicks on their Internet browser? I do — because Windows enforced the double-click action elsewhere in its OS to prevent accidentally doing something with a single click. The result is we lose that real-world connection between "hear a sound" and "get a reaction," which means extra learning, not less.

• Speaking of the Internet, remember when all the links were blue underlines? That was the way of things when the Internet was young, and we needed a visual reference as to what was live (clickable) and what wasn't. Here's the annoying part: We still need to know where links are supposed to be! But graduates of the Internet design schools don't want to look dated, so leaving off the underline and hiding the colors becomes part of a "cool" website (Groovy? Neat-o? Rad? Woke? Yet another example of needless change!) In the real world, underlined text represents something important. Not so on the Internet anymore.

• Bad=Red, Good=Green. Like the blue Internet underline, colors can be vital clues. We know about traffic signs and lights, so the color red is pretty familiar everywhere as a warning. Or is it: I once had a banking transaction canceled because I avoided the red button and pressed the other one. But the company's colors were red and white, and so the OK button was in red! Cultural issues and disabilities like color blindness mean we have to be cautious about using color, but when we do, don't reverse or radically change its meaning in the program from what we're familiar with.

If you look around, you'll find many places where the world has already trained your expectations. Carry these representations over into your programs, and users get a bit more knowledge at no extra charge — and your programs end up easier to learn for newbies.

#53: Remember Handicaps, Preconceptions

A problem occurs when building on one idea in order to explain a second idea — what if the first idea is not well known?

Traffic lights give us a well-understood alert system — until you encounter a user who isn't aware of the Red/Yellow/Green pattern. Or is color blind. Or is totally blind. And so on.

Take the red Exit sign — in some countries it's green (or if you're in one of those countries, the sentence should read "Take the green Exit sign — in some countries it's red.") Rely on a red or green exit sign icon to leave your program (and programs have used that) and you're guaranteed to confuse someone — not a lot, but some.

Obviously, if you're in North America, and your program is destined for just the North American market, you have less adapting to do. Red works fine here. Until it doesn't: Red-green color blindness affects about 8% of men, and 0.5% of women. That's 1 in 12 men who have to "make do" with your red color metaphor, and 1 in 200 women.

So is there a solution to reach everyone?

• Keep internationalization in mind at all times (also disabilities). You don't have to make every program completely international, with string sets for each language and such unless that is your goal. However, if you always keep in mind that different countries use widely different ways to describe things, you're less likely to get caught. For example, in French Canada an exit sign is red, but reads "Sortie" not "Exit." Better to stick to changeable text than an imperfect visual.

• Be ready to change. Keeping the big picture in mind, staying flexible and open to changes, will make it easier to reach everyone. Take the (in)famous Chevy Nova. In Latin American countries, "No Va" means "No Go" — a poor name for a car! Flexibility would have meant a name change for that market instead of becoming a joke.

• Use the tried and true methods built into the operating system. Companies like Microsoft, Apple, and Google have spent a lot of time and money on just this problem. While they haven't solved everything, if you work with their way of doing things you've got most of the internationalization and disability issues covered. For example, someone with visual problems can turn on the high contrast screen display — unless you decided your program's custom color scheme was "to die for" and now everyone is stuck with it.

• Redundancy gets the message across. There's a reason that icons and text are often together. If someone can't figure out the icon, the text can be a prompt. If you use color, use something else to go with it in case the color becomes a problem. Double up, and you give the user twice the options to puzzle out what your program is up to.

Not everyone thinks like you (very few, actually). Trying to get them to won't help with sales of your program. But meeting them halfway (or even all the way) gives you a chance…

#54: Icons Are Stupid!

Quick — look at any program you have running. What does the Save icon look like?

I virtually guarantee that's it's a dark square with a couple of lighter squares on it; one across the top and a smaller one at the bottom.

And it means?

A floppy disc, with the label across the top and the sliding read/write window below.

Funny thing though: My computer doesn't have a floppy drive. My last computer didn't come with it. Nor the one before that. Sony announced it had stopped manufacturing them in 2011. True, we're dealing with about a quarter century's worth of history for the venerable 3.5 inch floppy, but since then, years and years of hardly anyone using a floppy disk.

Yet the Save icon on computers everywhere is a floppy disk.

How many times have you held your mouse over an icon until the text tip pops up, so you know what it's for? I can't speak for others, but most of them make little sense. I get the printer icon — for printing — but I really can't make out a printer from the icon without a lot of squinting. On my word processor, the New command is a picture of a printed (paper) page — which could work equally well for zoom, preview, or print (get the page onto paper, right?) And even if I go along with the Save icon's floppy disk image, it turns out to be just about identical to "Save As" and "Save Remote!"

Icons suffer from quite a few issues that make them really, really bad:

• They are often inscrutable. How do you represent Internet-related menu options? Woe onto the program that uses a spider web icon! Or the cloud, another bad image, since no data is really up in any cloud-like object. And don't forget about cutesy or gimmicky icons, like the data processing icon shaped like a funnel, because, well, it "funnels" the data. Or the zipper because the files are "zipped." The end result is icons that make no intuitive sense.

• Translate This! These icon examples highlight another problem: What should they be in another language? For example, in French a zip file is "fichier zip", or literally "file zip." But zipper, which is the icon, is "fermetures a glissiere" or "closing slide." Computer people are used to translating "zip" as a compressed file, but newer French users see the zipper icon on their computer and justifiably say "incroyable" (unbelievable!)

• Reliance on icons takes away reliance on text. Icons are bad — but a programmer may use that as an excuse to not include text descriptions, or hide them in pop-ups or tool tips. The text helps — the icons do not. But we think icons do, so we bury the valuable info.

• Once we start with icons, we can't stop. And the metaphors get hackneyed after awhile. Start with Save and we have to do something different for Save As, and like I mentioned, the icons look close and are just confusing. But we've created that icon toolbar on our program, so we have to fill it with something...

The next time someone suggests icons, consider just using the menu. Or allow the menu items to be dragged onto the toolbar to create icons — but I believe very, very few users will bother. Frankly, they are mostly ignored: It wasn't until I wrote this tip that I really looked at all the icons on my word processor. Previously, I'd just learned the key commands, or where the menu settings were. And I believe a lot of others will too. So do everyone a favor — avoid icons as much as you can, or at least put the description for them front and center so we don't have to puzzle out their meanings.

A GUI Is Worth 1,024 Words

#55: Get Design Feedback

People use your programs. So people should say something about your programs.

I once rewrote a program to fix a huge raft of errors. I recoded it with C++ classes, sped up the I/O, and reworked the GUI so the display was clean and easy to understand. And it took ages to get traction. You see, the old version was already in use, and those clients had a sequence of commands they'd memorized for their tasks. They had to learn the new workflow, and unlearn old habits. The result was that for them, the new easier design was actually harder to use.

Later on, I reworked another program. This time, I brought all the stakeholders into the room, and I rearranged the display while they watched and decided where things should go. The result was a GUI that made sense to both new and current clients, and there were few problems getting it adopted.

Programmers program. Some of us also design. But users actually work with the program on a daily basis, and eventually can spend more time on it it than we did creating it. No matter how good a programmer/designer you are, unless you know exactly what clients are doing with it, then you're working somewhat blind. However, there are ways to improve the situation:

• For some software there is the user feedback group of one — yourself. This could be why so many programs are a success when the head programmer also wants the program for himself/herself. I once wrote a music player I used constantly. As a result, I took great care to make it work especially well, because I was paying attention to all the feedback of my fan base of one.

• Solicit feature feedback. I've never been a big fan of this: Clients don't always know what they want, and between people who think they are helping you with bad ideas, and people that always hate this or that, but are never going to use the program, there's rarely a lot of quality feedback. As well, pressing for feedback (or incentivizing it, say with money or cookies) further colors the results, skewing things more in favor of people who aren't interested in the software, just the payment. Nonetheless, you may find a few gems of advice if you get the right people.

• Betas/Alphas. Sending the software out there is a great way to get feedback. However, getting people using and testing it is hard: After all, they are spending their valuable time working with buggy software. In contrast, most of us avoid problem apps if we can. Still, for software with a loyal fan base, you might be able to get a few quality testers. If so, treat them like gold. I once beta tested for a company that gave out a single jacket to the top tester (and no, we didn't get to keep the software). With that meager show of appreciation and their dismissive attitude, I refused to have anything to do with their software for years. So beware: If you can get testers,

---

value them, or risk losing the only people who care enough to use your product before it's fully working!

• In a perfect world, you could interact with users and watch over their shoulders to see how they work things out. Called usability testing, a person sits in front of the screen, and performs a set of tasks with your program while being recorded. Others watch from another room, but can't interfere. The taskmaster assigns the tasks and is there for help on really tough problems, but the idea is that a user should try to solve each challenge using only the software; any issues or failures show you where to make the product better. A usability test like this is the gold standard, and well worth it if you want a "home run" product.

The greatest software really isn't, if no one wants to use it. Don't make my mistake. Get feedback early and often.

#56: A Little GUI (Change) Goes a Long Way

As mentioned, write software in isolation and it's all too easy to end up with a miss instead of a win. This is especially the case with the program's visuals. Use an array instead of a hash table and clients might notice a slight speed difference. But change the corporate colors on the screen, or rearrange dialog text or edit boxes, and mayhem is assured.

The key is to start small:

• If an item really needs to be updated, then update it. But get buy-in from others, ideally users as well. And do a bit at a time, confirming frequently with everyone that the results are what they expected.

• Always, always, resist the temptation to fix it "just because" — because you can do it better, because you want to make your mark, because you understand the design better than everyone else, etc. It may or may not be true, but unless there's a real solid fiscal reason to improve the program, you are doing nothing to help the company's bottom line, yet spending a lot of time (and money) doing it — not a good way to ensure job security!

• Starting small also prevents you from hitting major roadblocks. Say you redo one dialog and find out that there is a bottleneck with the server. Or instead you redo all the dialogs at once, and the program becomes so sluggish you can't test it properly to find out if it's the server's fault. Which is more practical?

• Finally, small changes avoid upsetting people. The fact is, change is something we all say we want, but get really uncomfortable with in large doses. Don't believe me? Then why do elevator pitches always relate a new project to something people already know? If we truly wanted completely new and different movies, the most successful pitches couldn't compare themselves to previous movies — but they all do. Raymond Loewy, a major industrial designer of the last century, defined this as the MAYA principle — More Advanced, Yet Acceptable. New and different, but not so much that it disorients us or makes us too uncomfortable.

So try change slowly — the medicine is always easier to take in small doses!

#57: Design With People In Mind — Specific People

When you develop, what User do you have in mind? It's not a trivial question, because who you are designing for influences how you design. Write a program for your Grandmother and you'll probably make the buttons large with lots of explanatory text. The same program to impress your friends will likely have a lot of glitz and chrome on it — maybe even an animation or two.

Programming according to client profiles is a powerful way to focus your software designing. One way of doing this is with personas, or detailed user stories. It's not just for software of course: I keep an "ideal reader" in my mind as I write this (it's you by the way — congratulations!) Likewise, businesses try to figure out their ideal customer; or customers, since sometimes you need more than one customer type to fit the whole client base.

The idea is simple: First I figure out my target audience, then narrow it down to an ideal user or users. For example, say I'm creating a PVR program, which will be used by a wide range of customers. This means multiple personas, grouped around typical "types" of people:

• Group 1 is young people who want to keep a copy of a show they can't watch off the Internet; they are very comfortable with technology, but they don't record much, since they watch less TV than other age groups. We'll represent them with a twenty-something named "Kesha."

• Group 2 is represented by "Nathan," an older avid TV fan. He relies heavily on recording lots of shows to watch when he gets home from work, or on weekends. He uses technology, but only as needed, so he'll need clear instructions on programming the PVR.

• Representing Group 3 is "Margie," who is retired. She doesn't need to record as much (she's home all day and can watch most shows "live"). However she does record a few favorite shows to watch again and again. The last technology she bothered to learn was a VHS VCR and the remote control, so she needs very clear instructions, and a lot of fail-safe programming in case something goes wrong.

Can you already see how much easier it is to design for each of these people rather than a generalized "customer" group? If I listed required PVR features, I expect you'd be thinking right away about how each would be used by Kesha, Nathan, and Margie, and how to design for them. And by programming for these three people, you also cover a huge number of similar clients.

That's one quick attempt at making up user personas for a PVR. In a real situation, you'd spend more time interviewing and researching to figure out the exact groups. As well, you'd describe the personas in greater detail to make the people "come alive" in your imagination (and your planning).

Be sure to take the time and effort, since it's possible to pick poorly. Many companies have invested in fixing the wrong problem, or the right problem for the wrong people (people who aren't interested in the solution). There is a famous quote attributed to (but not actually said by) Henry Ford, "If I had asked people what they wanted, they would have said a faster horse instead of a car." You want to get the right people for your design personalities, people that match your customer base, as opposed to "just anybody" — those anybodies that may want a faster horse, but will never buy your new car.

Figure out your specific customer, come up with a comprehensive example or two or more, and give them a name. You'll be surprised how often a concrete client persona will jell decision making.

#58: Pretty Is OK, But Beautiful Is Wonderful

Programmers don't need to design, right?

Right. But maybe you should try anyways.

Design is important. Look around — how often are crappy designs really enjoyable? Well done design just "looks" right, and is well worth learning. Especially now, with so much software moving onto the Internet, it pays for you to be able to both style and program a web page yourself. If not, someone else will give you a finished design, and it will be a mess to instrument your code into it. After all, how many web designers know to add onclick handlers, or break up their CSS styles to make it easy to turn specific items on/off?

Of course, in many cases someone else is in charge of the layout, so you don't have a choice. But even then, a little design sense goes a long way:

• Learn colors. There's a reason certain colors go together, and understanding the color wheel is basic to getting those kinds of things right. For example, complementary colors are on opposite sides of the color wheel, and tend to look nice together; but of course that's not the only color scheme possible.

• Learn color values. You should know the RGB/HTML codes for some common colors — after all, when you see #ff0000 don't you want to know if it's a bright red or green? But also learn color mechanics, such as intensity, or saturation. Playing around with these values can give you some mighty nice color palettes. For example, high intensity colors look good on games, whereas lower saturation colors are better for more "mature" products.

• Understand balance and layout. Have you ever heard of dividing a picture into thirds? Visually, we find images more interesting if the main object is off center, as opposed to centered exactly in the view. There's other rules like that, which, when you understand them, can make designs much more appealing with even minor tweaks.

• Learn to edit images. A program like GIMP is a free way to edit bitmap graphics. There is always a need for a picture or two in software, like icons, screen shots with titling, background tiles, etc. Waiting for the graphics department to send you a simple image is time a-wasting if you can do it yourself in five minutes.

• ...And vector graphics. Simply put, bitmap images are made of pixels, while vectors are made up of resolution-independent codes (like draw a line this long here, a curve over there, etc). The result is that a vector can usually be resized with no loss of quality. A free program like Inkscape can help you with that. The advantage? Regular images get grainy as they change size, but vectors stay sharp, so for example a logo or a program icon can be easily resized to all the versions needed.

• View and review good design. When you see a program that grabs you, analyze what is pleasing about it. Over time, you'll find yourself critiquing more and more software — and getting great practice in figuring out what works visually.

• Learn HTML and CSS. If you're not an Internet programmer, you may wonder if this is worthwhile. But be honest, who isn't doing Internet programming these days? When I work on an Android app, it requires layout XML, which is somewhat similar to coding HTML web page layouts. Programs that ran on Windows for years are now getting web interfaces, and need designs to go with them. And JavaScript? You can't go far in it without some awareness of HTML/CSS, and JavaScript is front and center in developing for the Internet.

• Keep at it. Even if you plan to do only command line programs for the rest of your career, there are benefits in knowing more about design. It's all around us, so why not understand it better — and maybe do some of it yourself?

#59: Help(ful) Files Have Their Place

In discussing design, time and again I've mentioned the need to meet the user partway so they understand your design. That in a nutshell is what help files do, bridging the gap between what they already know about most programs in general, and what they'll need to know in order to use yours specifically.

Of course, they exist for other reasons as well:

• They give your documentation department something to feel good about. (Just kidding.) (Kinda.)

• They provide a place for the "last word" on what the program can and cannot do.

• They may include training material.

• Oh, and if you write it, it gives you a chance to add "technical writer" to your resume, and broaden your skill set — not a bad thing.

Help is vital to software: Just imagine how hard it would be to figure out a program's eccentricities without some guide. Or perhaps confirm a bug is a bug and not an "undocumented feature."

So what should help do?

• Help should help. Obviously — but is it so obvious? I've encountered a lot of docs in my day that were little more than dumps of commands and display features; not that that's bad, just incomplete. You need to add info on how to use the program. Of course, much of it needs to be tailored to the client: The help file for a typical word processor needs less training material than some apps, since most of us are familiar with that kind of program.

• Diagnostics are great. If your program ever makes a mistake (never may that happen!) there should be a reference message for it. After all, if the program stops, it would be a good idea for the user to understand any error message in order to continue — and you do want your clients to continue using your program, correct?

• It should be current. Nothing annoys quite like docs that don't cover the latest features. Scratch that — skipping ANY feature, old or new, is taboo.

• Be careful to avoid computer terminology. If your user base doesn't know what a popup is, or a tool tip, then you need it spelled out in more detail. And while some phrases are obvious to programmers, they aren't to other groups. If in doubt, ask someone who is part of your program's target audience if the term is understandable or not.

• ...But do use the right terminology. And while you have that person handy, ask him or her about what people DO expect in the docs. After all, if you're writing a program for grammar, and they want to split sentences apart to analyze them, likely they will say they want to "diagram" sentences. If they prefer that word, use it.

• Understand how people think. There are important principles in learning you need to learn. People advance from familiar to unfamiliar, so bridging the gap from old to new is fundamental to all learning. People have limits in memorization, called chunking, which means you should not give them too many things at a time to memorize. And so on. The science of learning is big, and applying that information will make your help files much more useful.

• Be redundant. Remember to repeat, mention it a couple more times — and then say it again, Sam. There's an old adage: Tell them what you're going to say, tell them, and then tell them what you just said. People are usually distracted and disinterested in software. So if for example they pay attention to half of the training, then we'll need to say things twice in hopes they get most of it!

• Watch our attitude. Even if they are interested, we might be bored and distracted. We are close to the software. They aren't. As a result, our docs might end up being short and abrupt since it's all "obvious," and end up missing details a new user vitally needs. So stick to it and cover everything, so they can as well.

• Limit your synonyms. Writers are trained to use synonyms to avoid sounding repetitive. Forget that. In docs, if your clients work with thingamajigs, and think of them as thingamajigs, then call them thingamajigs each and every time. If they're called thingamajigs AND thingamabobs, then use both names; but it's best to introduce the terms at the same time, use them both once, and then stick to one consistently.

• Limit your vocabulary. In your help files, avoid exotic words and sentence structure. Keep your writing at a high school reading level or lower if possible. A sentence that is hard to read, or uses big words, is a sentence that will be skipped — a pity if important information is in it.

• Write while fresh. Like many of us, you'll quite likely put off writing as long as possible. Don't. Not only is procrastination a bad habit, it means you'll probably forget details. If you can't write immediately, at least make notes — good notes! If you don't plan ahead, you'll might end up "winging it" on a tight deadline, and that's never a prescription for quality work...

#60: Moving Pictures Go Way Past Book Lernin'

Do I really need to prove that images and video are powerful in training, more so than the printed word?

OK, fine — YouTube.com

(He drops the microphone and walks away.)

Show me a library that gets the kind of viewership (readership) that site does. We start thinking visually from infancy, and although reading begins early on, it's secondary to images. No judgment here, just a fact of life (although since you're reading these comments in a book, I'm guessing you can figure out which side of the writing/video debate I prefer!)

Nonetheless, more and more people find video preferable to text for learning. It takes more work to create quality video versus text, but it can make a big difference in how many people "get" your program. Some advice however:

• Always provide a written option. If you've ever tried to learn something from YouTube, you know how slow it can be. I frequently drag the scroll-bar pointer around to the main bits rather than wait. Give viewers text at the bottom, captions, even a printed summary in the description box (or whatever is allowed/appropriate for where you place your videos, if not hosted on YouTube).

• More and smaller is better than fewer and larger. Digging through a 45 minute instructional video for one of its tips is not as much fun as watching a two minute video specifically on that tip. As a bonus, filming and editing smaller videos is much easier on you.

• Trade gimmicks for quality. Have you watched a movie where they jiggle the camera to build tension in action scenes? At least I think that's why they do it: Someone figures it's a vital special effect, while I figure it's a sad attempt to build tension in a scene that suffers from major sukkage. Do quality, and you won't need gimmicks. Get to the point, show how to do something clearly, and then end.

• Details are important. If you are offering a series, consider a (short) intro logo or labeling. Work to make the resulting video classy and professional. Look around at other examples in your field, and make notes on which ones come across good, and which don't. The difference should tell you how important quality is — and how bad the result can be if you forget it.

• Clean is the way to go. Ever watched a video where the screen background is — ahem — inappropriate? I have. Don't demo a program where the wallpaper is a scantily-clad manga character. Or your favorite star, either fully dressed or not. And watch the icons — people can (and do) zoom in. Better to use a separate user account with an icon-free blank screen in a neutral color to demo programs. That also goes for data used, like test files, images, or anything else that can be off-color or "blue" (ask your great-grandfather what that means).

• Audio is your friend. Speak clearly, and do not slur. Make sure the volume is even throughout, and loud enough for the video. Avoid background noise: Take care to make sure your microphone is not going to pick up key presses or mouse clicks, the computer fan, traffic outside, nearby wildlife (of animal or human variety) and so on. It's worth it: Listen to a few videos with muddy sound, or low volume, or background noise, and you'll be a convert to recording quality audio.

You may not go with video demos for your product. But if you do, do it right. Anything else will affect your product negatively; so much so I'd argue you're better off not doing visuals, than doing them and they're bad. You've been warned...

Where Imagination Meets Reality: Debugging Your Code

All code has bugs.

There, I said it. Your job is to get rid of as many as possible before people use your program. Debugging and testing helps find them, by turning over the rocks to show all those crawling critters...

#61: Understand the Problem of Testing

In a nutshell: Testing is HARD.

• It's hard to do comprehensively; every branch can add two (or more) choices, each path of which must be tested. Two branches that each lead to two branches that each lead to two branches..., you get the idea, the choices multiply quickly.

• It's hard on the psyche. Programmers are optimists, spinning digital gold out of digital straw (Booyah! Rumpelstiltskin reference). In contrast, testing feels pessimistic and adversarial, somewhat like vandals damaging a beautiful structure, or a graffiti "artist" defacing property.

• It's hard to get good training for it. Far too many programmers follow the "spray and pray" method — throw test data at it, and hope it catches the worst problems. Disciplined testing methods are not taught as often as coding is, which means testing properly is frequently an afterthought.

So, yes, it's hard. But we must do something. What?

• Avoid complexity. If a small function can be tested (somewhat) and a large one is harder to test, the answer is simple — write smaller. Break functions as small as possible/reasonable and as often as possible, so testing effort is reduced.

• And of course, code well. Cryptic code give bugs a place to nest. They can burrow in plain sight because the code is just too hard to understand. Bad code like this will be revisited many times as you try to fix errors. In contrast, good code is so easy to read and understand there's (almost) no place for a bug to exist. Good coding helps keeps weird bugs away.

• Random testing is good, but not great. We often think that random tests will catch the unexpected. True; if it does, it will be unexpected, but think of how rare that usually is. Even a small function might have millions of test cases possible. Say you want to test a formatting function that adds commas to numbers, but the routine has an off by one error — at one thousand, one million, and one billion it puts the comma in the wrong spot. That's three errors in one billion numbers. How good does random sound now for catching some bugs? The superior solution is to build in non-random test cases, using your knowledge of the problem. Right away, we'd add edge cases, such as 999 and 1000, and catch the bug immediately.

• Test before integration as well as after. I've mentioned Test Driven Development (TDD) already, where you write the tests before you write the code. If you test each of your functions before stringing them together (and of course, testing them some more after) you'll catch a whole slew of errors that are local to the function. Do it only after they're all together, and it's an opaque puzzle, a "black box." Then you're like a mechanic who's told "there's something wrong with my car," as opposed to "there's an oil leak under the engine near the drive chain."

• Keep testing. The test bed should be maintained and always present. If you follow TDD then the tests stay with the code permanently, and are rerun frequently. Breaking a test means code is bad and MUST be fixed immediately. Ignoring or commenting out a failing test is a sure sign the code is getting bad (or the programmer!)

• Get familiar with a testing framework. For years I relied on assertions and my own test framework. Now however there are already-written and high quality packages out there, so use one. If you aren't using one already then the xUNIT family is especially popular (JUnit for Java, NUnit for .NET, etc.)

• Use it! True, it takes more time to set up a xUNIT test initially than it does just diving into the code, but I find that's actually a benefit: Since you think more deeply about the problem as you think up the tests, the (eventual) coding will go faster, and better. Also, keeping the tests around and rerunning them means changes can go faster, since you'll get quick feedback if they break anything.

Remember that untested code is uncertain code, waiting for an opportunity to bite you on the tuchus. Keep that in mind, and you'll find that over time thorough testing sounds better and better.

#62: Elementary, My Dear Debugger

Forget Sudoku, crosswords, or studying Sherlock Holmes. The real puzzle solving is in debugging code.

Where Imagination Meets Reality: Debugging Your Code

Testing is about assuming as little as you can, and thinking like the computer — very, very literally. You need to work back from the bug and try to figure out what the computer did wrong to get there (that's not quite true; after all, from the computer's point of view it did everything perfectly, and YOU made the mistake).

Here's tips I've found useful:

• Debugging is sometimes like a scientific experiment — hypothesis, testing, results analysis, iteration, etc. Take a bug, work back from it, ask yourself what caused it, then add code that (hopefully) shows if your idea is right or wrong. Sometimes it's easy — something does/doesn't go like it should, and a test will immediately prove it. Other times, it's a cascade effect, where one glitch affects the next function, which affects the next, etc. If so, take a step back, and ask yourself — how can I "scientifically" prove what/where the problem is?

Say your program is failing to return the correct value, and you think a specific function is where the problem occurs. To prove it, perhaps you check before the call, then after. If that doesn't solve it, try other spots. In any case, you guess (sorry, hypothesize) and then set up a test (oops, experiment) to prove/disprove your hypothesis. If you have a good idea what the problem might be, this can give you quick insight on uncovering the bug.

• Use the divide and conquer method for error checking. If you remove some code, and the problem goes away, then you know that code has some influence. If you're using the IDE, you can just comment out code temporarily, then another piece, then another, and you may figure out the problem reasonably fast. Ideally, if you take a line out and put it back in, and the bug appears and disappears in lockstep, you've got it. Of course, not all code can be blocked out, and there is the possibility that removing the code will cause other bugs, or make the current issue "move about," but when the bug is a real pain, it can be a useful technique.

• Regression. Go back to your last stable release (you are using version control, aren't you?) and add in all of the new code in small doses, testing each time. When the program breaks you've likely just added the problem code.

• Avoid blaming the hardware. It's fun to pick on the machine. But face it, it's just following your instructions. Sure, there may be those rare occasion where a power glitch or cosmic ray actually caused a problem with the computer — but the programmer that depends on those rare occasions for answers is looking for excuses more often than not, and in time might be also looking for a job.

• Avoid blaming the other guy's code. A variation of the blame game is to attack the Operating System, any third party libraries, and the like. Here, it's a little different, since their software could actually be at fault (surprise!) However, even then I'd take a moment. The reason is simple: If you think it's the other guy's fault, are you going to continue diligently looking over your own code? Probably not. If you have a suspicion it's their problem, then test it — wrap a function call with checks, and see if the results match what you expect. I routinely put checks around third party code, just in case. But don't slack off checking your own code as well.

• Set up a clean test machine. Reproducing a bug is vital, and nothing messes up a repeatable bug like a non-repeatable environment. Even if only for the most difficult cases of testing, try to set up a stable computer to run things. I sometimes like to use a virtual OS, and then reset it after each run. It's great for errors involving assumptions in the operating system, like files or registry settings expected but not necessarily on the target machine.

• Test everything everywhere. Of course, a clean machine won't catch all the bugs. So be prepared to mix it up; programmer's computers, client's computers, computers with low memory and slow Internet connections, and more. In fact, for much of my programming life, I programmed on slower computers and caught bugs that would only appear to those owning computers of aged vintage, which is a great way to catch performance issues (at least, I did this until I got old and crotchety, tired of working on slow computers, and decided I'd prefer programming on powerful ones instead!)

• Be suspicious of the newly departed or the newly arrived. I don't mean employees (although there have been cases of fired employees sabotaging code); I'm talking about new and removed code. New code and new bugs, or new bugs and missing code are what we refer to as "high correlation" (well, I just did, even if no one else does). Checking those sections if new, or the routines calling the removed code (or the patching that bypasses it) can help you narrow down the problem areas, and maybe — just maybe — make short work of bug hunting.

• Do the walk. Code walk-throughs are very handy. Having others look at the code, or explaining the program to another person, sometimes might alert you to problem areas, and help you figure out the bug's source. Even just looking at code that might be at issue and mentally walking through it line by line can be useful.

• Understand that you will never catch them all. I was recently working on some code that I wrote a decade and a half ago. I immediately spotted a memory error that had never occurred, but would have been really bad if it had. Fortunately, other parts of the program had redundant checks that kept it from blowing up. I like to think I knew that when I coded it all those years ago, but I suspect not. Try to catch the ones you can, try to bulletproof and redundantify the remaining code (I made that word up — feel free to use it), but be humble and aware that others may remain.

#63: Tiptoe Thru the Digital Tulips

This mangled reference is old, old, old (I despair that any reader will have heard of Tiny Tim, but my Dad liked him — feel free to YouTube him).

Tiptoeing refers to what I consider an extremely vital part of code testing — walking through the code.

Almost all modern code tools allow you to step through your code, checking registers, the stack, memory and local variables, setting breakpoints, and more. Use that tool, or if you don't have one, find one for your system — it's that important. Learn it inside out, and then work with it:

• Eyeball code before running. I can't tell you the number of times I've forced myself to review code before running it — and caught something. Review a function ahead of time, and you likely will too.

• Always walk through every path at least once. You need to see what every line is doing. A walk-through is a game, where you check if the computer does what you expect it to — and then fix things when it doesn't. Remember: If you skip a branch, you have not tested that code. I regularly reverse flags in my walk-through just to confirm the alternate section (like error logging) works, and then reverse the flag back again. Nothing is quite as annoying as finding that the error logging code has an error in it at production time! (Note that I mention this, not as a good practice — which it isn't — but to show the need to test both sides of a branch. However, I risk making a mistake when manually reversing the test, and potentially introducing a bug. Far better to put in good test cases to test both branches without code editing, but oh for shame, I don't always do that. So do as I say, not as I do...)

• Some fans of TDD feel that the code tests are good enough, and you don't need to single-step line by line. I always walk the code anyways. When you single-step you learn details about your coding, details that will also help with future test cases. And being right there as the code executes is like having a front-row seat to the brains of the CPU, showing you exactly what it thinks of your code, and helping you code better and more precisely the next time (especially when it hiccups on code you thought was fine!)

No matter your testing discipline, I recommend "breaking" the debugger out — you'll gain from the experience, I promise.

#64: Legacy Code Needs (Testing) Love Too

Inherited a program with no tests? Legacy software without builtin tests is a real bear to work with. Not only is there no way to be sure the code won't break with a change, but functions written without tests are often quite dense and hard to instrument (add tests to). So job one is to get some tests into the code. What to do?

• Keep externals external. Buried globals in code are always annoying. If your function calls a global inside, then testing that function means you need the global too. But if your function instead passes the global as a parameter, then you can test by passing other (testing) values in place of that global. You probably won't always be able to pass external values in parameters, but if you can rework the function to do so, a test harness for it becomes a lot easier to set up.

• Slip in indirect test code. Externals aren't just variables of course. Say you call a database from within a function. Is DB testing impossible? No. Move the DB calls into a separate class, and then pass that class as a function parameter. For the regular program, the real DB class is passed to the function; for the test class, pass a custom DB class (for example, an in-memory DB you set up yourself). The function still calls a DB, but now you decide which, externally.

• As much as possible, control the test environment. The real-world DB we just talked about could have anything in it, but our custom in-memory testing database must be set up exactly the same each time. Otherwise, you're not just testing the function call, you're actually testing multiple random interactions with data. For example, say you accidentally leave off the WHERE clause in an SQL DELETE statement, which means it will delete every record. If you use "just any old" database, you might use one with a single valid record, which won't catch the error. But one with proper test data (multiple records), will catch this. As I've mentioned, random values are not as good at catching bugs as we'd like to think, and you're better off doing specific tests. Control the environment, control the tests.

• Mocks and stubs are your friend. Networking functions? Internet calls? No easy way to test them reliably, even if you put them all in a separate class, since networks are unpredictable. Unless — a test version of that class has dummy calls that do the bare minimum (they don't even go out onto the network!) Called mocks or stubs, the idea is that the code does only what's needed to make the test run and pass.

Say you're worried about not opening/closing/reading a file properly. So your mocked up **Open()** might simply set an "open" flag. Then **Close()** would clear the flag. No actual I/O goes on, just checking the flag in each function: **Open()** would make sure the flag was false ("true" would mean it's trying to open an already-opened file), **Close()** would test the opposite, while **Read()** and **Write()** would check that a file was open. These calls are simple to write, but end up testing the I/O for only the problems you worry about, with little modification to the legacy code, and no dependencies on actual I/O.

The testing becomes even simpler if you had passed the I/O functions as a special class or parameter: For one set of tests, these file I/O class stubs would just test this flag; for another test, a different class might do actual I/O; and so on. Swap in specific stubs, and test exactly what you need.

Don't like extra function parameters? Use inheritance, where an I/O base class is called within the function, and you swap child classes in as needed for testing (say, with a preprocessor or compiler directive, or via your testing code setup function).

It should be clear that all these tips depend on inserting a layer between the current program code you want to test, and the parts you have little control over. That little extra layer gives you back the control, and makes the code much easier to test, often with very little adjustment to the legacy code, and the risk of introducing bugs with the changes.

#65: Don't Hide Intermediates

One way to make testing easier is to keep intermediate stages of a calculation alive.

For example, I used to try to get everything for a calculation into a single variable — bonus points if the calculation result could be RETURNed directly, saving me a variable assignment.

Funny thing though: Every time I walked through those sections of code, I needed to add a variable to check the calculation results. It took far too long, but it finally got into my head that it's easier to create an intermediate variable or two and leave them in the code.

Why "waste" a variable like this? Because if you ever need to check things out, you can just break right after the value and view it. For complicated calculations, walking through each step lets you figure out when and where a bug appeared. The small cost of storing partial results can make a huge difference in debugging later on.

Another benefit: A large, monolithic formula is a breeding ground for bugs. Break it into manageable pieces (and by that I mean pieces you can wrap your head around) and the going gets easier.

Oh, and it makes testing easier, since you can test intermediate results. For example, if you needed to add X degrees to a temperature in Celsius and then convert it to Fahrenheit, break it into two calculations, one for addition, and one for the conversion, and you can `assert()` both results (not necessary with such a simple example, but you get the idea.)

Resist your ego here. I can tell you from experience, the fun of saving a variable or two is quickly dissipated, especially when you look at it ages later, and curse the younger you for being oh-so-cryptic in that code. Old cryptic code sucks.

#66: Leave No Bug Un-Understood

It's quite simple: If you don't know exactly what you fixed, how do you know if you fixed it?

We've all been guilty at one time or another of spray and pray coding — tweaking values in code until the program runs. It's quick and dirty, and sometimes it actually works.

And you should never, ever do it.

The same goes for spackle coding. That's where you have a bug, and you just patch the code to fix the error, not the real problem. Got an error when the value is equal to zero? Just add a test for zero and return another value — problem solved! Why was it zero? Who cares, it's working now!

By now you understand, bugs don't go away, they just hide until the lights are off, or the client is in the room. And frankly, if you don't know where it goes, and of course, where it comes from, that pretty much means the whole program is suspect, right? Not a vote of confidence for that piece of software...

So always, always, always, understand the bug. Follow every error until you can see how it's happening and where. Set up tests and trials to make the bug show itself. And when you fix it, check that the result is as expected (this is where stepping through the code is so valuable).

Train yourself to get annoyed if you can't explain exactly what the bug is and why it exists. Let every error you track down become a lesson you internalize to help you catch the next one. That itch to solve them will make you a better programmer. And a popular one. After all, which programmer does a company want — one that spackles code problems, or one that cuts out the rot and replaces it with quality coding?

Even here, there are exceptions: As adamant as I am about understanding bugs, sometimes I've used spackle coding for a last minute demo or when the time crunch is on for a code release. But I've fixed it as soon as possible. And no, I'm not proud of it. Don't you be, either.

#67: A Repeatable Bug Is a Fixable Bug

The worst bugs are the ones that appear "sometimes." Sometimes bugs are really hard to fix. You can't get at them directly, so you're trying to patch anything you can in hopes that it solves the problem. And if the bug goes away, is it because you fixed it, or is it just waiting for an opportune moment to reappear?

Clients get sometimes bugs a lot. They are often accompanied by partial information about how they appeared, and never enough details (to be fair, the client's job probably doesn't include monitoring our software for usability).

How can you get better information so you can reproduce the bug?

• Get the word out that if you can see it, you can kill it. Get everyone on board understanding that identifying it will help you, and therefore them. Any extra information or details, what was going on, what happened next, and so on — all of that can make a huge difference.

• Talk. For the bad ones, an email or support ticket won't cut it. If possible, a call to the client is in order. Sometimes in conversation key details will pop up. I once had a tricky bug where the program just up and failed, with no clues why. Digging around in the code provided (as they say) No Joy. Eventually, in conversation with the client I was able to find out the steps they took to get to the issue, reproduce them locally, and finally used all that to kill the bug dead. There are lots of details that never make it into a support ticket, details you may really need with a tough problem. So talk.

• Log like crazy. Logging is a skill, since no one wants 100 megabyte log files every time they run their program. But if the bug is buried, you'll need some form of state display. So grab as many of the internal values as you reasonably can and dump them into a log — often. If you are very, very blessed, the log might show a variable going twonky just before the bug hits, making it easier to narrow down when and where the problem occurs.

• Do a program divide and conquer. Clients hate this, but putting together a dumbed-down or partial program lets you eliminate sections of the code from consideration. For example, if the bug is in the display, you then get rid of three display routines, and the bug goes away, then it may be one of those routines. But not always: Maybe those three routines just delayed the program long enough for a thread error to crop up (ah, threads again!) It's a bad form of divide and conquer programming — far better to do this at your own location and testing setup — but if their site is the only place the bug occurs, you're stuck. Sometimes desperate times call for desperate measures...

The best bug is no bug at all: But if you're going to have one, at least try to make it repeatable.

#68: Document Bugs, No Matter How Embarrassing

So you found the bug, and fixed it. Now what?

Document it — always. Even if it's YOUR mistake that brought on the bug. Especially then.

There's several benefits in doing so:

• You're going to make mistakes; the key is to not make the same mistake twice. Documenting it reinforces the solution (and problem) in your head. The act of reviewing the bug sharpens your memory, improving the chances you won't code a similar one in the future. And if it's someone else's bug, you'll now know how to avoid it without making it yourself, a bonus.

• The mind is tricky — paper isn't. Despite what I say about remembering bugs better, we are all infallible. As well, programmers leave or move around. So someday in the far, far future, someone will be glad you detailed the bug, how to reproduce it, and how you fixed it. Of course, that bug will never happen again (right?), but perhaps another one will appear like it. Or a "fix" breaks your fix and the bug is released once more into the wild...

• A database of bugs reports is powerful. Part of programming experience is getting used to what works, and what doesn't. After a while of recording bugs, you'll develop a sense about them, and be able to zero in on them faster. Believe me, that sort of experience is very, very welcome; but it comes by learning from mistakes.

• It can uncover a pattern. If a lot of bugs are coming from a certain section of code, documenting it will bring it to your attention. From there, you can consider rewriting that buggy bit, or doing an intense code review of it.

• Honesty is always the best policy. Being candid about mistakes has, in my opinion, always worked to my benefit. True, I've risked getting my tuchus dumped to the curb, but hiding mistakes never seemed to be the best policy. Your mileage may vary, but I suggest that owning up to errors, no matter how bad, will in the long term tell your employer you are a stand-up company man (or woman) — after all, if you don't hide your painful/embarrassing mistakes from them, you're probably not going to embezzle or steal office supplies, right?

So for every bug, remember to write, right? Document it and then you can forget it — just never completely of course!

After The Fun Is Done: Maintenance

Programming is great. Well, writing code is great. Maintaining code, um, not so great. But it's necessary, so this is about how to deal with that.

#69: Lists? Check. Checklists? Double Check. Or, How to "Remember" to Do Everything Right the First Time

Surgeons use them. Airline pilots use them. So why not you?

When you put software together to ship, any of a huge number of steps can be skipped if you're not careful. A list takes care of that. And whereas egos everywhere have complained about following lists, people still use them — because they work.

A checklist for a project isn't as life-threateningly vital as one for surgery or airplane landings, but it is important in your business. Imagine shipping the wrong code, or missing documentation, or keeping the test harness enabled. Ouch!

At the very least do a step by step guide on how to package and ship your product:

• Bump up the version number, and do a production compile, removing any non-production code or test harnesses. And always turn off debug mode.

• Package the code properly for distribution, be it an installer, .ISO, .ZIP, or something else, and also check and double-check the package. By the way, that also should include generating checksums. For work in Windows, I can create and send a file checksum that the receiver can verify via certutil.exe:

```
certutil -hashfile "{YOUR PATH}\file.ext" MD5
```

• Always virus check. I like to run the checksum, then virus check, then run the checksum again. If the package includes an install program, I virus check the installer, install the package, then virus check all the executables it installs — you can see where a checklist helps keep this straight!

• Make backups — a lot of them. I like to backup code before I process it for shipping (before the debug flags are turned off, production settings turned on, etc.), as well as the code used to make the package, as well as the final package for shipping, as well as documentation, as well as…, you get the idea. Backups are cheap. Recovering because of no backups is not. And ALWAYS more than one backup. Bonus points for getting one of those backups offsite immediately, say within a day or two.

• Test the final result. Ideally, grab a clean computer, do the install, run it, and watch for problems. Something left off the install? Then uninstall and reinstall, using a different destination directory each time. It's not perfect (Windows registry keys aren't cleaned up, for example), but it catches many install issues.

Yes, it's a lot of work, and after fixing multiple tiny last-minute errors a half-dozen times you'll wish you didn't have to ship. But being obsessive-compulsive about the final product, and using a checklist, has saved my bacon many, many times — and it will save yours when you use it.

#70: Perfect Is the Enemy of Good Enough

Perfectionism can kill companies. There is always something else to do to make a project "perfect," and programmers love to tinker. After I've finished a program or key function, I'll lie awake at night thinking about things I could add to it, ways to streamline the code, rewriting or refactoring that would make the code easier to maintain, and much more. I'm guessing you do too.

It's great to want to improve your code, but resist it strenuously near the end of a project:

• Real artists/programmers don't dawdle, they ship. Talk to an artist and you'll hear how there is always something else to touch up in a painting, drawing, or whatever they create. But it has to go, or no one gets paid. Likewise, the goal of software is not perfect, but sales worthy, and unless you can profit from it, you'll have a tough time programming for a living.

• Don't rock the boat. Tinker now and you risk redoing a lot of work, so consider carefully. One excellent way to bring this home is to handle all the testing and packaging yourself. After hours of minor changes and repeated checking and installing and testing and repackaging, you will hate your code. Now take a moment to ask yourself: Every change from now on will require that whole packaging rigamarole again. Is it worth it?

• Watch last-minute changes. Perhaps a variable should be renamed, or a comment improved? Frankly, if the code is kept clean throughout the project, this should be a really rare case. However, if you have to, remember to use the IDE's refactoring for safe variable/function name tweaking (for example, to prevent errors with ordi-

---

After The Fun Is Done: Maintenance

nary search and replace changing only parts of other variable names), and make sure comments really do enhance the code, making it clearer for the next person. But remember, renaming a variable or two and adding comments near the end is not the same as major code refactoring and adding features!

• Balance is necessary. If you come in the next day with a form redesign that improves data entry efficiency 300%, that's worthwhile. But if you think a salmon background looks better than light cocoa, that's tweaking that few will care about. If in doubt, mention the change and rationale to your manager — if he or she agrees to it, you've likely got a real improvement.

• Keep your perspective. All those pretty code internals that we like to slave over? When was the last time someone said, "Thanks — I can really tell the difference when you replaced that hash table with a dictionary" (or vice versa)? Outside of programming circles, if the code gets the job done, few care about what's under the hood. I recently saw an ad promising 65% faster clipping or whatever in a new version of an art program I use. So what? I didn't realize I had a problem with my current version's clipping speed. I suppose if clipping took 30 seconds, I'd appreciate it now working in 10 seconds. But I think it's only a second or two. And if it was a problem, I think I'd remember, so it isn't, 'cuz I don't, see?

Having said all this, I want to point out I'm not talking about shipping shoddy software. The program should work, and work well (perhaps the quote should add "Real artists ship — QUALITY"). But any little extras you feel compelled to add that won't impact the program significantly? It's sometimes called gold-plating, and like gold-plating, it's cosmetic but doesn't change the fundamentals. And especially when you're on a time crunch, it's well worth skipping — at least for now.

#71: We Don't Need No Stinking Backups?

(Wikipedia "stinking badges" for the reference to this heavily butchered title.)

I've already covered this a little in a previous tip, but it really needs its own point: Do backups. A lot of them.

I remember when floppies were used for backups. One 1.44 meg floppy craps out, and 25% of your 5 meg program was unusable. Which really meant 100% of your 5 meg program was unusable. So you got in the habit of making multiple backups.

Then came CDs. Goodness, a whole 700 meg to store data! Now you could store two copies of code on the same disk — sometimes three — and there was still room for documentation, test code, even the compiled program or installer.

DVDs stretched that further, with 4.7 gig (8.5 for a double layer disc). Should be enough, right? Yet somehow now we produce code that won't even fit on an itty-bitty USB memory stick — the dongle has to be at least 16 gig to be useful. Of course, with that we can store whole compile environments, install images, all the testing data and documentation, and more. But it highlights how much a programmer's backups have grown. And more importantly, how fragile they are.

I fear for programmers who cut their teeth during the CD/DVD eras. Those discs really felt permanent (They aren't: I recently went through some fifteen-year backups CDS with multiple read errors). But USB sticks? Now THAT is fragile. I've had several of them fail on me over the years, from twonky sectors to the entire USB's electronics giving up. And whereas a 1.44 meg failure was bad, losing 16 gig is far, far worse.

On, and the Internet? Sure, you can backup files out there ASAP; no waiting until the bank opens to put your files in a safety deposit box. But you may worry about your data being stolen, or corrupted, or peeked at, or a host of other things. Given the amount of hacking out there, somehow storing gigabytes of data on the cloud feels a bit risky (not to mention the time spent uploading). However, if you go that route, check into the security offered for your files by your cloud service, since it pays to understand the worst before it happens, not after.

But cloud or USB, local or offsite, what is the key to everything? Redundancy:

• At the minimum, use 2 or 3 memory sticks.

• Backup to each and confirm all files are there with a file list tool. I like to create a complete copy image on my computer drive, then check it carefully, then copy the whole image over, then check again. At a minimum run a checksum to confirm all the files are there and are correctly written. Use whatever tool works best for you, but use something (one free option is the fciv.exe program from Microsoft's site).

• Store one dongle in a safe place (safety deposit boxes are great) and one local for emergency recovery. If you have a third one, consider storing in another safe location far, far away from the nearby Tsunami or earthquake or forest fire or ice-age glacier zones (that is, whatever your local area fears most in terms of disaster).

• Rotate carefully. Keep at least two generations of backups away from your site. I'd even be cautious and keep some permanent offsite backups, say once a year or so, that never come back. All it takes to ruin things is one unnoticed file to be corrupted, with that error uncaught for a few months until you've rotated all the good copies back to the shop and overwritten them with bad ones. USB drives are cheap: Recovering corrupted or missing data is not.

• Check and recheck. Not only checksum the memory sticks before and after, but do a full scan on them before use. If there are bad sectors, a complete low-level format should get them (not a "quick format"), and reduce the risk of a device going bad and corrupting your data on it. For critical data, even consider making two copies of it on the same stick.

If this sounds paranoid, it is — and frankly, the best programmers are paranoid.

#72: Embrace Clean Running for the Next Time

Now that you've shipped, it's time to breathe and do some damage control: If your computer failed today, how soon would it take you to get back to work?

In my case, I have a second computer ready, with an operating system installed, and have a backup of all my product logon passwords. In theory, I could download or otherwise install all the software I needed, upgrade my tools, and be ready to go in a day.

In reality, I've tried this in the past. It always goes far worse than it did in my imagination. Perhaps I forgot to note a password update, or I use a special program that I can't find anymore, or it has exotic licensing (such as linking to a specific computer's hardware). Maybe the test environment has a bunch of little hacks I've used over the years to make things smoother (like setting up a link to the command line on my desktop, or taskbar links to my design tool), but forgotten to document. Or after some software is installed, it needs a huge amount of time to update to the current working version.

If you can spare the time, I'd recommend doing a dry run. Pretend your main computer is down, and see how switching over goes. The goal is to get a complete production environment set up for whatever code you're working on; ideally, for every single project you have, in every language, and with every tool and all the testing data you require. Then put it together and go through everything, just like you would on your main computer.

Expect it to be painful. It's strange how annoying even little changes in the environment can be. I once worked on a keyboard that had a narrower-than-usual Enter key. Years later, I frequently hit Enter instead of the Quotes key; my finger's muscle memory still thinks the Quotes key is farther over to the right than it is. Change is hard, and darned annoying.

But you can anticipate it and be smart. Note what you'll need, then evaluate what to do different when the time comes. In my case, I've promised myself to use less proprietary tools, since moving the licenses can be a pain. I'll try to package more together, for example keeping code and test beds in nearby directories, to make transferring and backup less painful (and to encourage me to backup more!) In some cases, I'll try to put everything onto a virtual disk image, and then just copy that from system to system (although again, with Windows the proprietary aspect is a pain to manage).

When they say in the movies "this is not a drill," you know it's about to go really bad for any unprepared characters. Practice your drill ahead of time, and you

---

might be annoyed when it happens for real, but that's nothing compared to how you'll feel if you aren't ready.

Seeing The Big Picture: Project Requirements

Before there was code, someone felt a need, a need for code. The need usually ended up in the form of requirements and specifications. But not always. So it pays to understand when people turn their desires into your code, just in case your next program's full specification is handed to you on the back of a napkin.

#73: Battle Plans Never Survive the Battle

Over-planning can get you into trouble. Don't get me wrong; sometimes you need to specify everything in detail (did anyone say government contract?) And of course under-planning is a very, very bad idea. But if you micromanage each detail in micromanaged detail, then like the quote says, parts of it won't survive the first skirmish with the enemy (in this case, our otherwise-beloved computers).

There's also more problems:

• Rigidity in design means little flexibility. What if you've promised everyone that one screen will do the job and then find out you need two? A more flexible design document ("approximately 1-2 screens of information") will likely keep everyone happy and prevent complaints.

• Programmers like to innovate. Too much detail inhibits that, and leads to frustrated programmers. Imagine you have a team of programmers that work strictly from specification. Are you likely going to get (and retain) wildly creative programmers with a rigid spec? And if you do, are they encouraged to try new things, and if they try them, will they be incorporated in code if they work better than the current solution? With your spec carved in stone, I think the answer to each of these questions is obvious.

• Micro-managerial thinking can prevent nimbleness. Steve Jobs said "real artists ship." Real developers, too (who by the way see ourselves as artists). And in the rush to ship you sometimes need creative solutions, like figuring out which feature to scale back, or how to give 90% of the functionality with only 60% of the code. Again, inflexible and overly detailed specifications can steer people away from creative thinking when they most need it.

#74: Don't Prototype Yourself Into a Corner

I once wrote a demo of a program in a language I was comfortable in — Visual BASIC, in a shop that was coding in C (to give you an idea of the time, it was Borland C and pre-Dot-Net Visual Basic, I think version 4). The demo worked well, so well they demoed it at a trade show.

Then we had a problem. Replicating the demo in C was not simple. Customers hadn't lined up with open checkbooks, so there was no idea if there was a market yet. And adding features to a demo took time away from fixing current software (my actual job). So in the end we had to move on, and leave the prototype alone.

Prototypes can make a real difference for a small company trying to make a splash, but they have gotchas:

• Prototypes can lock in specifics too soon. Because I did my example in VB, some functionality was unique to that language. Playing audio at the time was simple for VB, but much harder to implement in C. And management, unaware of the differences, would have been frustrated by the length of time spent rewriting for what they perceived was a simple language change.

• Write it as well as you can right away, because there will be lots of changes. This is where your computer science courses will come in handy. All that object-oriented stuff? Really important when you are designing a program that does X today, but Y tomorrow. Code everything so it's well encapsulated, a black box; and keep the linkage as lean as possible. That way, when that editor has to move from a local Windows form to an X Window server, and then to the Internet, you won't have to redo as much of it as if you'd coded all those screen calls directly. More thinking upfront means less work changing prototypes.

• Build it as if it's going to get big, because it often does. There's nothing management likes more than a program with lots of features. Features mean more things to hook customers. This is good. Unfortunately, it means that the code could blow up in size with the many, many add-ons — if you're fortunate and get customers all excited to buy it. So try to spend a decent amount of time putting a good foundation in, so you will be better able to expand the program later.

• Consider throwing one away. Use a prototype to get client feedback and interest, then put all that plus all that you learned from writing the prototype into a new program. If you can get management on your side, the result will likely be a cleaner, more robust program, since it will incorporate all your latest knowledge, but without any of the dead ends and discarded features that crept into your prototype code.

#75: New Is the Enemy of Time

You have this new library that will make your program run easier and better. Or your boss wants to try a different language for coding. Or you've read about a complicated new algorithm that will speed up things tenfold or more.

No problem, right? Wrong. Anything new is unexpected and can impact the timeline, sometimes horribly. It's vital to monitor how changes affect your deadline:

• In software, there's often a time crunch already. Adding a new item will blow up the schedule. Even a small item is rarely small, once the whole time cost of including it is factored in.

• Set a time limit. If the new code needs to be working in a month, what will happen if it isn't ready? To estimate how it's going, what test can you pass/fail in two weeks? One week? By midweek? If you can get a clear answer as soon as possible, you can change to other options without sacrificing too much time.

• Beware of icebergs. For example, a library has a small API to learn. But there's a lot hidden under the surface: Using that API requires reading the documentation, studying a lot of examples, and being aware of exceptions; or worse yet, finding them in the wild when your code doesn't work properly. Much of the issue in using new products is figuring out how big that part hidden underwater is. Try to minimize the unknowns ahead of time: Read the docs, check out the samples. See how much buzz there is online for it. For example, if every question you ask requires a lot of digging on the Internet for answers, be aware that it'll be the same once you start programming with it.

• Paradigms are shifty. New paradigms (ways) of doing things often mean learning something new, and learning something new is going to take time, time you'll likely have to take from other activities. Can you remember when you first learned object-oriented programming? And the time it took to really "get it?" If the program/library/code/technique you're going to use is a paradigm shift, be aware of how much time educating yourself on something radically new will cost you, and decide if it's worth it right now.

We all crave novelty. But novelty in programming usually equates to extra time spent learning, and so unless you can spare the time, be careful not to "byte" off more than you can do...

#76: Nothing Is as Constant as Change!

Change is inevitable. For the programmer, change is always something to be managed. However, the key time to watch for changes is right near the end of development. How so? If someone wants a feature at the beginning, no problem; just add it into the spec. Likewise, feature requests slated for the next (future) version give you time to plan.

But the ones that come around the end of the project are the tough ones. Sometimes a client has a request: Sometimes management or sales has got an idea in their head. In any case, time is of the essence. With a deadline looming, what should you do?

• Understand you'll pay the piper, someday, someway, somehow. TANSTAAFL is an acronym for the old adage "There ain't no such thing as a free lunch." Every addition or change requires coding, testing, possibly redesigning and rewriting promotional materials, and much more. A pushed-back deadline can impact the bottom line, shareholders, and jobs. Somewhere there will be a payment required: If the change is worth all that, then fine, but be aware — and let other stakeholders be aware as well.

• Embrace the idea. The automatic thought with any change is "Oh No" (or worse). However, two problems with that: One, the idea may have merit, a lot of merit, and adding it could enhance the program and make things better for you in oh-so-many ways. Two, if you go negative you create a mental barrier to get over. Like a little kid that doesn't want to eat their veggies, things get slow and annoying and the big people will get upset. Embrace it however, and you start looking at ways to implement it, possibly in a fraction of the time that any grousing would have taken.

• Understand that adding water to a pot risks overflowing. Whoever wants the feature has to be reminded of the fact that time is a fixed resource, and an extra feature risks shoving others back. Let them make the decision if possible. Here is also where a positive attitude works in your favor: If you have a history of acting in the company's best interest, your manager will know your arguments about time aren't a cop-out, but a genuine risk assessment. So it's quite possible they will act on it.

• Learn from the past. A schedule slips? Take note of why. Next time, if relevant, use those notes as concrete examples of what will happen, and therefore what not to do. You aren't in a fight with management; you're on the same side. But they have a slightly different vision from yours for the product, so it pays to keep your examples ready in case they forget the past.

• Prioritize, rank, and organize. Understand where a feature is coming from. Is it a nebulous sales feature, or a solid feature the program (and customers) really need? Will it takes dozens of hours, or is it a quick adjustment to a single routine? Is it so vitally important that it must ship with this version, or can it wait for the next one? Whether you realize it or not, you are already ranking every request. Sometimes it's based on whether you like the person, if they asked nicely, and so on. But practice ranking on more impersonal reasons, especially how they affect the bottom line. By balancing the requirements and requests in this way, you'll focus on how important items can move ahead more easily, and hopefully keep everyone happy.

• Modify, add, and remove. When you prune or evaluate feature requests, it pays to look at alternative solutions. Can an option have an extra setting or two, thereby getting rid of a complete extra feature? If you add a more generic option, can a couple of special requests be combined? And so on. If done right, a little thinking like this can save a huge amount of programming time.

Remember the "tyrannical trio" of development — work can take a specific amount of time, resources, or cost — pick any two, and expect the third to shift itself around. Understand that you'll never completely control all three, and plan to always play triage with requirements. So learn to do it well.

#77: Be Aware of Incomplete Requirements

"I want it to do this."

THAT is an incomplete requirement. For example, "I want to fly" is also an incomplete requirement. The airplane is one result. So is a glider. So is a swan dive from a diving board, or slipping on a banana peel (length of flying time was not specified).

The problem is that a broad requirement is hard to pin down. Imagine a multi-million dollar contract for flying that ends up with a cannonball into the local pool — and a statement that the contract has been fulfilled, so pay up!

A good requirements document needs sufficient detail in it:

• Support is NOT optional. It's a rare (I'd say imaginary) program that can exist without a single question asked about it; so what kind of support is expected? A website with a popup helper app, along with tutorial videos and a managed forum, is not the same as a README.TXT file in the product's directory, or an incomplete FAQ on your blog. Especially for larger, more complicated programs, the level of support is significant — and needs to be planned for.

• Tell don't ask. You may not have this option in many cases, but if the client (or programmers, if you are in management) aren't sure of the path to take, recommend — firmly — one that you are familiar with, and that you expect will work best for all (you are up to speed on your project, aren't you?) If the management doesn't have an opinion on something, and you do, you might end up taking a load off of someone's shoulders.

• Put a document together. Have every stakeholder involved right from the start in actually specifying the details. This does two things: Gets the project discussed before coding starts, and deals with issues people may not be aware of, because they haven't actually thought through the project in detail.

• Communicate. Take the earlier flying example: Even if people got together for an hour and were asked "What do you consider successful flying for the purpose of this document?" you'd get much more solid answers that trying to put something together on your own. Get them involved, and then really listen to their views.

• All together now. I strongly suggest involving everyone as a group, to make it harder for someone to tack on extras later. Some people like avoiding the meetings, so that they can come in later and say "Why wasn't I included in this decision?" It's a power play, so whenever possible nip it in the bud and keep everyone in sync.

Even a simple document can make a difference. Like the old story of the blind men describing an elephant, everyone has their own opinion of what your project is — based on their point of view — and they aren't likely to agree on the details. So before you start is the time to nail that all down.

#78: Measuring is Vital to Planning (and Finishing)

Ever heard of "Measure once, cut twice; measure twice, cut once?"

That second measurement reduces the chance of error; but have you ever wondered how many mistakes someone made before they came up with that saying?

Cutting a board wrong is a shame, but usually not too costly. Measuring the output of a dozen person programming shop, then using that estimate to guarantee a program can be ready for Christmas sales, is a much more expensive thing to get wrong. Therefore, learn to measure really, really well:

• Here is the price of this book in one piece of money-saving advice: Look at the end goal and work backwards. If you need something by July 1st, then work back to today and estimate how much each part will take. Keeping an eye on the end goal works wonderfully to focus your planning.

• Here's the price of the book again (now you've effectively got double your money back!) Measure small, not big. Each of your milestones should be short and measurable, with plenty of them. Think of it this way: In a six month project, what happens if everyone is slightly slower than expected, say 10%? After six months, the project is about 2.5 weeks over schedule. But if you checked every week, then after week one that 10% is only one half of a workday extra, a much easier error to recover from: Tweak the schedule, get more people, adjust features, or whatever, and get back on time. The next goal, you adjust again. And so on. Shorter goals give you more time to assess and recover from problems.

• Beware the programmer alone in a room. Measuring also includes that lone programmer: Someone doing "something" needs to hit milestones like everyone else. No one likes it; but what if after six months you found out he/she has written a completely different section of code than what you needed? It happens far more often than you might think (or perhaps it's already happened to you). Everyone must have milestones that are checked frequently.

• Include some buffer space. No plan is perfect. If you can overestimate here and there, you'll appreciate the extra padding when a feature runs long — and something invariably takes up too much time.

Measurements are vital in hitting software goals. As they say, if you can't measure it, you can't improve it. Especially for programming, if you can't measure it, you risk never finishing it.

#79: Keep Track of What Works For You

Our memories are BAD.

Last week's itinerary? When we graduated, or moved, or ended our last job? Heck, what was lunch yesterday? Took a moment to remember, right?

So given that, how do we learn and improve? By noting what works and reviewing it in permanent form.

In programming, you may have heard of an end of project code review, or postmortem. No matter the format, or how formalized it is (or isn't) in your company, do something as a summary for each and every project. Get everyone together to reminisce how it went, and note the pros and cons down somewhere. What problems occurred, and how could they be solved next time? What went right or wrong, and why? The goal is not just to review the project, but to glean what can be repeated, avoided, or done right in the future:

• Take the computer language, for instance. Did the choice of language help or hurt, or make little difference? On the one hand, the team was likely familiar with it; on the other hand, perhaps the tools or libraries you needed didn't mesh well with your code.

• The same applies to methodologies. Reasonably, every project should be an attempt to do better than the last one. So if Scrum or TDD or UML or Waterfall model worked, note it; but if it wasn't perfect, or you think you can do better, those observations and reasonings are invaluable here.

• Teams? Some grow together and work well, some don't. Did the team you worked with jell into your ideal dream team, or did it fall short? Who would you have/not have on your next project, and why? You may not be able to do anything about it, but it's always good to have an answer ready if the right person asks.

• Tools. Not just whether the tools you used helped do the job, or whether there were problems (for example, not enough time to get up to speed with them); you also want to know if there could be other, better tools used in the future.

• Time. OK, you never have enough time. But are there aspects that come to mind? For example, did a last-minute feature push the timeline? Did a "death-march" mentality make it difficult to keep alert and focused (assuming you were ever really awake once the march started)? What can be changed to remove or reduce any time crunches in the future?

• No accidents. Accidents don't count here, unless you can quantify and repeat them. For example, getting a star programmer for two weeks from another project may be worth noting, but it's only actionable if you can get her/him again for the next project.

• Do it! Even if you're not head honcho on the project, you can make notes. And the benefit of personal notes is they can be as targeted and specific as you want, discussing people or things that will help or hurt in the future (politely, of course).

As they say, "Those who cannot remember the past are condemned to repeat it." Take notes, learn from them, and then the past can stay history for you.

Seeing The Big Picture: Project Requirements

Dealing With People (Repeat After Me, A Programmer Is Not An Island)

Ah, the days of coding alone in your room, doing software the way you want it, when you want it! Once you need money, those days start to fade away. And people rush in — too many people. Arguably the hardest part of a programmer's job is dealing with people even when you don't want to. But whether you're in the trenches or management, interpersonal skills are vital. So here's some "people" tips to keep in mind.

#80: Code Is Clean, People Are Messy

In programming, absolutes are routine, and things are predictable and regular. Two plus two is four, and even 1.0 can be handled if you keep round-off in mind.

But people? Now that's a toughy. Depending on your level of social skills, you may find this tip full of new truths, or old hat:

• Some people lie. Or if you prefer, they will fudge, misstate, inveigle, confabulate, and more. In many businesses, people start with "what's in it for me," and go downhill from there. Your job is not to improve people or educate them in being honest and compassionate (at least I've never read that in any job description). Your job is to play with the cards you've been dealt.

• Some people try to avoid work, unless it suits them. And even that is an exception, since a programmer can often redefine work to mean a pet project that interests them, whether it is exactly the code that is needed or not ("get that GUI finished" can easily morph into "I needed to optimize the display buffer for the last two months.")

• Negativity abounds. This is most noticeable when you get a lot of "Nos" or "You can't" when talking about specs. I've found that many "You can't do that" comments were really "I don't want to do that" in disguise. Saying no is an easy way to lighten the workload — far easier than saying yes, which invariably gets you a new or enhanced assignment, and likely more work.

• There are many, many agendas. People rarely are focused on the company's success, but on theirs instead. Not that that is bad necessarily, but if you interact with people, you have to remember that the way to get things done is to accommodate their specific needs and wants if at all possible.

• You are on your own. To the extent you and someone else's goals align, you can work together. In some companies, that can be almost everyone. But in my experience, there is always at least one person in the group that looks out for his/her self. Usually, that means throwing other people under the bus to get ahead — and it isn't long before everyone feels a target painted on their back. While business friends can be great, be cautious.

If this tip sounds cynical, my apologies. I wish I could tell you that life is all rainbows and fuzzy kittens, but more often than not, in almost every business there are people who want more, and that usually means someone else has to give up something (whether they want to or not!) So be alert, because ignoring the problem isn't going to make it go away.

#81: Be Nice

Everyone should have a moral compass. Sadly, some ignore it, or avoid it, or maybe never had it in the first place. Hence the previous tip.

But don't be one of those. Nice is underrated, but it can be powerful:

• Be nice both to those who matter and those who don't seem to. Some people like being snobbish to the "lessers" — after all, they seem to say, why be on top if you can't rub their noses in it? But nice pays: The receptionist you chat with may one day turn out to be married to the boss (true story). Or maybe dining with that co-worker no one else wants to eat with ends up tuning you on to a great new Chinese restaurant (also true). You may find some people have more power than you expect — or will be advising people who do have it.

• Find/Create options for mutual gain. So-called "win-win" scenarios are hated by some people. Let that never be you. Try to figure out how both sides can benefit, and then get people on your side by being on their side first.

• Be cautious. Of course you can't do win-win every time. Some jobs require someone to be on the losing end (job assignments, for example). And there are people who know that, and so are busy planning to get the advantage. Try to spot those problem people quickly, keep a paper trail (more next), and refuse to get involved in their games. It's not always possible to be Switzerland; however, one advantage is that those kind often make lots of enemies, so by simply avoiding contact you might end up way, way down on their hit list.

• Keep a paper trail. Being nice doesn't mean being stupid. Be aware of problems, and like the problem-solving maestro that you are, ask yourself what the worst-case scenario is, and then solve for it. And be ready with documentation, notes, plus whatever else proves your side of the story. Obviously, this works best if you have a sterling reputation, otherwise they can have notes on you! One word of advice: Just because you keep notes doesn't mean you have to use them — perhaps consider them a "nuclear option," a last resort you may not be able to come back from, and keep them ready for those extraordinary times.

• Develop a thick skin. "Slow to anger" is a useful philosophy, especially in the computing world. I personally think the ratio of ill-mannered to normal people is the highest of just about any occupation I've encountered. Let immature behavior get under your skin and you'll be upset constantly. Work on staying calm, and you may not stop everything from happening, but you'll keep your blood pressure lower while it happens.

Oh, and that reminds me: Being nice is good for your mental and physical health, too.

#82: Learn to Communicate Well

Have you ever watched a really great speaker? Someone who can not only use words effectively, but can motivate, educate, entertain, or whatever else the goal is?

Be that person.

Communication comes in many forms: The written and spoken word, visuals in presentations and graphics in programs and online, and more. It can even be in the way you dress: For example, if your goal is to communicate a certain level of success, you can imagine how you'd dress, can't you?

The point is that every aspect of your job benefits by some form of communication. From comments in your code to emails to help files and help documentation to specifications to blog posts, presentations, and beyond, this tip is about getting others to understand what you have to say:

• Learn the mechanics well. Not just spelling, grammar and enlarging your vocabulary (all of which are vital), but also how to communicate a point, or explain yourself, or persuade others. You only have to look online to encounter really wishy-washy writing. Be the person that states a point clearly, cleanly, and effectively.

• Speaking well is vital. "Well" is defined by your audience, by the way. There's an interesting story Gene Simmons of the rock group KISS tells. As a young boy newly moved from Israel, his accent was definitely not American. So he sought to change that by imitating TV Newscasters, which in his day had a predominately Midwestern accent. Newscasters speak to appeal to their audience, so he hit on an easy(ish) way to appeal to most people — don't speak in an accent. At least, not one

---

the local people can detect (if he'd moved to Australia I suppose "Shout It Out Loud" would've had an Aussie twang!)

• Throw in some public speaking. You will eventually talk to a group, possibly a large group. Learn to speak well. As someone who has done public speaking from a very young age (six — seriously), I can tell you it gets easier with practice. Today's younger crowd has no problem in the spotlight, but if you're an exception, find a way to improve, like joining the Toastmasters.

• Read about writing. Books abound on any aspect of writing you may need, from grammar to business proposals to sales copy — and much more. Get into the habit of reading some how-to books, and applying them whenever you can. Bonus: Books about writing help with speaking, too.

• Practice. Take on communication jobs whenever possible. And review constantly. If you give a speech, try to view a video of it. If you write something, have a trusted friend or two offer critiques. While it hurts to hear about mistakes, fixing them early on means you'll have fewer of them down the line. Plus it helps to develop a thick skin…

#83: Expect Part of Your Job to Be Educating

If you are a manager, you'll often find a big part of the job is explaining — explaining to management why some things can't happen, explaining to programmers why some things MUST happen.

Think of the job as translator. For example, many bosses think in terms of feature sets and saleability. Many programmers think in turns of algorithms and "neat" features. Therefore, to help a project move along, you might be able to reframe a programmer's pet idea as a benefit to customers, and a valuable sales feature as an interesting programming project.

Maybe.

Other times, there may not be a simple solution. But sometimes explaining things properly can be simpler with a bit of care:

• Meetings. Of course, try to get out of them if they are not relevant to you. Arguably the worst time waster, they really impact your efficiency. However, if they are necessary, prepare well. This can be a great chance to educate everyone, and get your points across.

• Be accurate and precise. For example, talking about a project can often turn an "I think" into an "I promise" that you won't find out about until much later. Solution? When you open your mouth, avoid generalities and anything that may appear to be assent — unless you ARE agreeing.

• If you don't specify it, you're not going to get it. Or put another way, what you get is not what you were hoping for. Again, be clear: Leaving things to interpretation rarely means yours!

• Bad ideas can come from anywhere, but beware of those from superiors. An idea from above shouldn't be dismissed lightly (ideally, no one's ideas should be dismissed, but let's face it, some ideas are more directly linked to your paycheck than others!) It may be uninteresting, or hard to implement, yet not bad (say, a vital feature). Other times, the idea might stink. Stepping back and understanding why it's bad is important so as to explain yourself well. After all, if you can't explain why it won't work to yourself (time constraints, physical impossibility, cost, etc.), then how can you convince anyone else? You have to understand the problem first in order to translate.

• Be an authority, not authoritative. Nothing screws up morale like "Because I told you so." It doesn't work well coming from parents, and it works worse from managers. If you have to make people do something, it's much easier to take if you can explain accurately why, and back it up with facts and/or logic.

#84: Managements Woes

This is not a management book — but in managing people I've made enough mistakes to know what I should have done better, so feel free to learn from them:

• Beware the sloughoff — a programmer with an agenda of his own. You know them. Their code is always "almost ready." They work odd hours, with almost no supervision or accountability. The job they do seems to take far more hours than reasonable. Likely they are the only one who can maintain the code they are working on, so management is resigned to their idiosyncrasies. The easiest solution is to get away from them as soon as possible. But if you have to face them, then try to get someone shadowing them so there is another programmer who knows their code. Once that is in place (and I make it sound easy — it won't be, as this kind is often quite good at sensing threats) then some of their power and leverage is gone, and you can start negotiating a change in their attitude and habits.

• Move programmers around occasionally, so they develop new skills, and you aren't stuck with a single programmer who knows key code (the previous issue).

• Train for the greater good. The company must come first, and individual programmers are secondary to the business being successful. That sounds cold, but let's face it: Every programmer would prefer a paycheck from a still-functioning company than nothing from a bankrupt one! Therefore, the purpose of developing programmer's abilities and training them is firstly to maximize their benefit to the business. Of course, the programmer has input in this: After all, sending an unmotivated programmer to a course is likely a waste of money. But if you have several programmers all wanting to go to a course, pick the one that will give you the most "bang for the buck," such as a proven willingness to apply what they learn, or an eagerness to come back and share the knowledge, thus getting you extra staff training on the cheap.

• Programmers estimate according to their own schedule. This isn't unique to programmers of course; for example, everyone finds annoying tasks take longer than fun tasks. Motivation matters, and a programmer irritated by something will be in the programming slow lane, and in the fast lane when they are happy. As well, projects that get them notice from upper management, or bragging rights among their peers, will get some programmers positively drooling. And so on. What to do? Try to figure out what makes each programmer in your group tick. Remember, you're not out to change them — they're adults — but you're just trying to find the best fit between the code you need and their goals/motivations.

#85: You Manage People, Not Projects

If you manage, you may think you are managing projects. You aren't. By now, you might have realized you are managing resources, and one of those resources is people.

Don't believe me? Imagine getting rid of all the people under you. Same project, same deadline — just no way to hit it!

Of course, no one gets rid of their staff like that. Or do they? A bad manager can get people to leave (or at least want to leave) as fast as little mousies leave a sinking vessel.

So since people skills are vital to your project's welfare, keep these points in mind:

• Be prepared to give and (especially) receive counsel. It's easy to tell people to do more, and do it better (at least, if you're at the managerial level I'm guessing you find it so; otherwise, job #1 is to learn how to manage employees effectively!) But more often than not you will find issues come up when delivering that advice. No one is perfect, and so you'll occasionally have someone taking offense, or telling you how to say it better. Pay attention, and apply it. Not only will you improve in how you handle people, but nothing rallies the troops like a general who can take criticism just as well (or better) as they can dish it out.

• Treat people with respect. This can be hard with the problem people, and let's face it, they are the ones you'll likely be dealing with most often. However, they deserve the same respect as your boss, your fellow managers, or anyone else in the company. Be careful, especially if you feel like your opinions are more important than theirs, since it can cause you to overstep boundaries. Valid criticism is hard enough to accept: But personal opinions from the boss that carry the weight of "rules" are far harder.

• Don't pit people against each other. Parents sometimes play their children against each other to get them to do more. It's a nasty practice in a family, and it's worse in a company. Favoritism can drive people ahead, but at what cost? I realize that many managers will disagree with this one, but I stick by it. Get people to do the best because of their desire to do great work, not to beat out the next person. You'll end up with much better employees in your department.

• Take the blame instead of passing the buck. Some managers have an endless scapegoat list for every project, so someone else is always held responsible when there are problems. Ironically, those same ones often have no one else but themselves to thank when the job goes well! Don't be that person. The (bad) buck should stop with you; the good is spread around the team. If that seems skewed, well it is — but that's why you get the manager's salary! Block everyone from the rain, but let them bask in the sun, and you'll have a happier and more motivated staff.

Agree or disagree with these points, but managing people is vital to think carefully about — so ignore this at your peril!

The MBA Side Of Things: Programming As Your Business

Wherever you work, whatever you do in the programming field, you are in business, the business of YOU. A Master of Business Administration degree (MBA) covers an education about the business side of things. And let's face it, who doesn't dream of being their own CEO or founding a startup? So these tips are relevant for just about everyone. After all, over your career, you'll likely wear many "hats" in your jobs: Might as well learn to wear them well!

#86: Underpromise+Overdeliver

How many times have you seen a movie that was over-hyped, and went away disappointed?

Too often, I imagine. But how often have you gone to a "sleeper" and went away thinking it wasn't too bad?

We have expectations, and if they are high, there's a risk of disappointment; too low, and we can be pleasantly surprised.

So start low, and give extra:

• It's not just a sale, it's a relationship. These days, a sale is often immediately followed by the salesman heading out the door. Viewing each sale as a chance to do a little extra can catch customers by surprise. Being there for your customers after the sale will be more work, but the relationship building really makes a difference, espe- cially in a fickle economy where everyone changes vendors at the drop of a hat (or sticker price).

• Give as much as possible. Offer them product promotions, tie-ins, giveaways. No matter what you do, you'll stay in the client's memory, and that's important. Do you have a local furniture or clothing store with "Crazy" in the name? Watch their

---

promotions. They don't do them because they are crazy — they do them because they work.

• Consider the price of underselling, or even free. I say "consider" since this has the potential to be abused, but some companies can get a foot in the door doing a little loss-leader sales. Evaluate if you can afford to do so, but if it's for the right customer, it can make for a long and profitable relationship.

• Sell, sell, sell. Always advertise your company or yourself. Always be selling your product to potential customers, and never let up. Your goal is for them to see you as the best solution to their "pain," whatever that pain may be. People don't buy detergent because they like it — they are annoyed by dirty clothes. So be the soap they need.

• Keep busy. Nothing says "active business" like frequent updates (unless they are fixes, which can backfire if they are too often!) Frequent updates, especially with new features, have a couple of benefits: Competitors are forced to play catch-up, and if you slip in an interesting new feature from time to time you also keep your clients enthused. After all, who doesn't like something extra for free?

You are a business, even if only a business of one. Give'em more than they are expecting, and they'll love you no matter your size.

#87: Be Aware of (But Don't Follow) Sneaky Corporate Tricks

I've said before, I'll say it again: A lot of people out there are not nice.

If you program, and only program, you may not need to know about this tip. Your boss and CEO will deal with those kinds of people. But if you are a manager, or self employed, then it pays to be aware of some of the worst tricks out there:

• FUD sucks — but it's common. A nasty trick from a company is to spread FUD (Fear Uncertainty Doubt). It can come from many arenas — a big company promising a new product that causes all the smaller companies to give up; patent trolls threatening litigation unless they are paid; smear campaigns about a new feature or product not being very good; and so on. Basically, it's using press to scare and worry competitors. It's a cheap shot, easier than coming up with a superior product, and not classy (on the other hand, how many companies thrive on saying "we're the classy ones?") If you experience this, one option is to evaluate then and there if your project is worth it. Even better, consider both possibilities — if their threat materializes, or if it doesn't. Then think long and hard if it's worth going ahead.

• Using standards. Did you know standard aren't necessarily free? MP3 is a standard — and until recently, it cost you quite a bit to use that standard. The people who come up with the standard (in this case, the patent holders) stand to make a lot from people who use them. They are also good for monopolies. Think of software requirements for operating systems (like "logo" programs) and realize that a company offering standards or certification is pushing a wheelbarrow to the bank — and it's overflowing with your money.

• Embracing standards, kinda. What could be more fair than everyone sharing a standard? Unfortunately, a company can accept a standard, then come out with a version of it, but with just a few tweaks. They don't have to be better, just different. Then promote like crazy. In the end, this second version muddies the water, confuses everyone, and splits the market in two: Standards-compliant, and one non-compliant competitor.

• Submarine products are bad. You know the kind: Submerged and pretty-nigh invisible until they float up and shoot torpedoes at you. Remember GIF? A free and open format for images, or so we thought. Then the Internet got big. Then the owner of the patent wanted money. Then it got really messy. Then we got PNG images as an open solution to the problem. MP3 was another one — lots of Internet code on how to play an MP3 audio file, and then a patent group contacting you when you tried to publish anything. It all looked free; but of course, that was the point.

So be aware of anything that might be turned into a costly problem for you — because given corporate greed, it probably will be.

#88: Trust No Supplier

If you have influence over your company's supply decisions, keep this one in mind: "Always have two suppliers."

In the business world, working with real objects instead of code, it's common. There are scads of stories about companies that become the sole supplier to a business of a specific product or part, and then things went bad:

• When a company realizes it has you locked in, the temptation is to raise prices. Not every company gives into temptation, but many do. And the cost of finding a second supplier on a time crunch (and it's always a time crunch) is never worth the few percent extra the prices are raised — which is exactly what the supplier is counting on. And even if the supplier is genuinely needing the increase in prices, it's still a good idea to be ready with options.

• It pays to look at the worst case scenario. Nasty suppliers may be rare, but ones that go bankrupt are out there too. Or ones that phase out a package, sell it to another less-friendly company, or change the license. Then what will you do?

• Especially for programmers, you should never get locked in to learning one library, code base, or compiler if you can. Your career is tied to your specific knowledge, so if say 80% of that is with one company's product, that's a lot of your eggs in one very fragile basket! Companies come and go, and so do products. One exception is if you find an Open Source solution that you can use forever without extra fees. But even then, expect many, many changes, including ones that might break your older programs (look at the changes in Linux desktop environments over the past twenty years).

• Be aware of how expensive "FREE" is. I'm not talking about Open Source (although it is possible to get caught here, since Open Source does not have to mean free for commercial use). I'm talking about tools and libraries that are free now, until they become popular enough that a company can swap a new license in. The catch with this kind of free is that the price inversely affects the value of it: You think it's a good deal, and often give up researching others because "the price is right."

I had this happen recently with an audio license. Totally free and without restrictions. Until it wasn't. I soon realized that legally I couldn't use the old code anymore, but using the new would get expensive fast. So an enormous chunk of time spent learning went down the drain by walking away from the project. On the bright side, if they'd waited a month or so to release their license, my code would've been live, and I'd have been stuck with a license I didn't want. Morale of the story: Beware free, since it doesn't have to stay that way. And as a side note, ignore how nice people are when they offer free — they're nice until they don't need to be nice anymore. Cynical I know, but that's business.

• Let me repeat — be very nervous when your code base is tied to a specific "something." Constantly ask yourself what can go wrong, and also how much time can you expend to look at alternatives. This might involve getting one of your team to explore competitors' solutions, coding options in-house, or investigating if there's another less-risky license (for example, a perpetual license with source code).

Have a backup plan for everything you don't own outright or control totally. Not all solutions are possible, but evaluating whether a problem with a company will be an issue is like insurance on your house: Do you spend a bit now to avoid risks later, or do you skip it and hope nothing big and bad ever happens? Finding an alternate source for everything is well worth it to reduce that risk.

#89: Understand Where Customers Are REALLY Coming From

In a perfect world, customers eagerly want to buy your product, and there are no problems. In the real world, they don't always, and there are many problems:

• Some customers want, but aren't fond of paying extra for it. For example, an offer of "add this feature and I'll buy" should be backed with an iron clad purchase order. If not, you could find yourself with an expensive new feature, and a potential customer that changed their mind. Then what are you going to do with it? Maybe you just "eat" the expense of development; or perhaps you add the feature to the main program, and that customer ends up with it for the regular price. Of course you have to balance this, since sometimes great programs out there were created by pivoting for a specific group of clients, before that first purchase order was signed.

• Some customers aren't. Imagine you are a competitor. How hard would it be to slam the competition online by acting like a customer? Very easy. So a customer that contacts you about a problem should be able to discuss their contract or supply an order number, otherwise you may be helping a competitor posing as a customer to rile everyone up.

• Pay attention to complaints. One estimate is that for every complaint you actually hear, fifteen others complain, just not to you. I think that number is way too low nowadays, but the fact is few people will complain directly to you about a problem — but they will complain, and complain loudly. So analyze the ones you get carefully, just in case they reveal an issue that others can (and will) have.

• No complaints? Big problem, especially these days, when everyone has something to say. No complaints could be a sign that a product is just not reaching critical mass. Think of it this way: If people find a problem, unless they care enough, they'll just move on to the next app. And if they do care, they know complaining is the way to (hopefully) get results. Therefore, no complaints could mean no one cares. A million downloads where no-one gets past the splash screen is no better than zero downloads (worse even, if you pay for the bandwidth!) Frankly, if no one has anything to say, you probably haven't annoyed them enough — and everything annoys somebody these days.

#90: It's Your Business

You're smart — but there's a lot of other smart people out there. And they have their best interests at heart, not yours. In no particular order, here's a list of advice that might help you in the business aspects of your life:

• Residuals are good. Generally for most people, you work, you get paid, and you're done. Or, you can do the work and get a royalty paycheck for a long, long time. Guess which one you'll be glad of twenty years from now? Keep your eyes open for the occasional work that pays in royalties, and it can add up.

• Sales are king. Simply put, the greatest program without sales is not the greatest program. You need money to live. So as much as you may feel that programmers are the most important people in any company, you'll have to make room for a sales team. Or get really good at selling.

• Only fools get net. That's an old line from movie studios: Through creative bookkeeping, a movie could be hugely successful, yet not have enough to pay everyone. Search on "darth vader not paid" — it turns out the actor never received royalties for "Return of the Jedi" because it (technically) lost money! Gross is the total money coming in, while net is what's left after all the bills are paid; and as this example shows, a creative accounting team can find a lot of bills, and make the net disappear entirely. While you likely won't get a net versus gross offer anytime soon for your software, it does highlight the importance of reading contracts over, and asking yourself — what would a nasty lawyer or accountant do with this deal if they could?

• Sell razor blades. A very old sales tip is to give away the razors, but sell the razor blades. That idea has become a bit muddied since disposable razors came on the scene, but the key of it is that the big money is in supplies, not equipment. Sell a car once, good money. Lock them in over the life of the car for all repairs, maintenance, rustproofing, oil changes, etc — great money. In software, think subscriptions, or apps with in-app purchases; now you understand why they can give those programs away for free.

Hacking Yourself

It's nearing the end of the tips, and I close with a few more, aimed squarely at the most important factor of all in becoming a better programmer: YOU.

#91: You Change, We Change, They Change — Embracing the Inevitable

The thing about getting old is that it's only with years that you can see some things clearly — and then the young don't want to hear it!

But just in case, here goes:

• The language you use now will change in time. Quite possibly you won't be using it in ten years, or twenty. Prepare for learning a new one — or likely a lot of new ones. Being able to ramp up quickly in a new computer language is a great skill to have, and future-proofs you.

• As technology changes, it will need new and more specialized coding for it. For example, I remember a time when you had to draw a line on a display with integer math for speed; now, graphic processor chips are so common that you can re-purpose them for bitcoin mining, and no one programs low-level graphics drawing anymore. But there's new work if you know how to program graphics processors for bitcoin mining…

• Technology is moving faster and faster, and it takes effort to keep up. So be the one that gives 100% effort, and you'll quickly pass people doing 50%, 70%, even 90%. Read, learn, practice. Keep growing and you'll become a moving target: Remember, moving targets get hit less!

• Try to go broad in your learning if at all possible. As time goes on, more and more people will have to narrow their focus because there is just too much to deal with and learn. In contrast, the generalist will become rarer and rarer — and therefore more valuable.

• Always keep alert to developments. Be ready to change direction and follow new ideas that have potential. Internet Of Things. Artificial Intelligence. 3D Printing.

Cloud Computing. Big Data. Many of these terms didn't exist, or have changed, from ten years ago, and will likely change much more in the coming decade. But by paying attention to trends, you might find one you want to be a part of, possibly well before the majority notices. And that could make you quite valuable as an employee or business owner.

• Practice predicting the future. Review past ideas to train yourself to anticipate new ones. What about the iPhone? Facebook? YouTube? Twitter (OK, not a good example). But could you have guessed how they would go right from the start? Not likely, but now armed with those examples, could you do so with a new product in the future? Practice, and you might end up dead right on one — and one is all you need!

There will be many, many changes in your life. Keep aware and alert, so you will be poised to benefit from those changes.

#92: Ergonomics and You

My wrist hurt.

I had just moved to a new office, and all of a sudden my wrist hurt — a lot. I was seriously considering carpal tunnel as the culprit, and worrying about surgery and my programming future.

Then I thought a bit, took a look at my surroundings, and realized my posture had changed. Before, I had an el-shaped desk that let me rest my elbow, so less stress on my mouse hand. Now, no el in the table, and my hand was hanging over the desk edge, actually pressing right on the wrist. Immediately, I practiced holding the mouse at a different angle, and within days the pain went, never to return.

Do you have eye strain? Sore back? Funny feelings in your legs when you sit too long? Pay attention! Pain is the warning message that you're doing something wrong, and the sooner you figure it out, the sooner the pain will go — and hopefully stay away, unless you take too long to listen to your body's warning messages.

Look around your work area, note issues, and act fast. At a minimum:

• Exercise. Even a little can make a difference. For example, sit-ups pull in the stomach, which reduces back strain. Getting up and walking occasionally improves circulation in your legs. Many people recommend leaving your desk at least once an hour for a short break, even if for just a quick walk about the office.

• Look to your lighting. A lot of talk is out there about blue light and how it affects sleep cycles, or fluorescent lighting versus full spectrum lights. As well, too much/too little light can strain our eyes. Uneven lighting can do the same: I once had my desk briefly facing a window, and the bright sunlight peeking over the monitor caused huge eye strain within minutes.

• Location, location, location. I've mentioned my mouse, but where you place your monitor, how high your chair is, your keyboard position — in fact where any of your equipment is placed — can all affect how you feel. For example if you use your printer a lot it makes sense to position it close, rather than strain to reach it dozens of times a day.

• Switch it up. Ever tried a standing desk? A walking desk? Perhaps a ball chair or kneeling chair? These devices may take getting used to, but you might find one that helps with a specific problem.

• The air that you breathe. At one job an employee ran his car to warm it up at the end of the day — right by the fresh air intake for the building. Trust me, fresh air makes a huge difference in thinking ability! Also, pay attention to how well you breathe, since sitting in a chair is a poor position for deep breathing; if you find your breathing shallow, you'll likely see that lack of oxygen reflected in your coding before long.

• Involve your company. Clearing up issues like this in the workplace can have a real impact on your productivity; so your boss has an interest in helping you figure out the problems as well. Get him/her involved. After all, a fix that improves your productivity (say) 5% is small, unless it also helps 20 employees: Then you've effectively added 100% productivity, almost like hiring another employee — but at no extra cost!

Changing things up in your work-space can make a huge difference in your feeling of well-being. Sometimes it takes a bit of detective work (like my wrist) but the rewards are worth it: Better health and less (or no) pain when working. So keep alert to issues and seek to fix them quickly. It's trite, but true: You only have one body, so take care of it.

#93: Learn to Manage Your Life

We all have 24 hours in a day. But some people can make it look like five, and others, like thirty-five. How? By controlling your life, rather than having it control you:

• Learn to manage your time effectively. You need time to play; managing it well will leave you that time — probably more than if you just try to wing it. Rich people hire chauffeurs, which gives them extra free time when commuting to work. Some send their laundry to cleaners rather than do it themselves, and effectively gain time every week. Get the idea? Even something as simple as reading a book during lunch makes your time more productive, and frees up more time to be spent elsewhere — time to be enjoyed, hopefully.

• Health matters. Sallow and pasty-faced may have been a "in" look for programmers in the 1990s, but today we're smarter about health. As mentioned, exercise helps you at work; but a healthy body also improves and lengthens your life. The catch? You actually have to do something. No amount of fancy meal plans or gym memberships will help unless you take charge. Make it as much a priority as any other aspect of your life; after all, it IS your life we're talking about.

• Handle risk properly. One big thing in life is risk. Some people love to live life on the edge. Some don't. Here's a trick — spend some money you can afford to lose and buy a stock. Any stock. Then leave it. If it goes up, do nothing. If it goes down, do nothing. See how long you can last. If you go nuts when the stock drops, expect risk to be a big issue throughout your life, and plan accordingly!

Depending on how risk affects you, you may need to buy that house while young for security; or you may have no problem quitting your job and traveling the world every few years. But the time to know how much risk you're comfortable with is before you get a thirty year mortgage, or hand in your notice.

• Get organized. Use a program or paper lists, or perhaps your mother calls you and reads off what you need to do every day. Pick a system, any system, but rely on it. Puzzling over what to do next can kill mucho valuable minutes in a day.

• Think about goals. If you know you want to be a young CEO, how likely are you to take five years off to live on a beach in Thailand? On the other hand, if you don't know what to do, Thailand does seem nice... But one goal might make you successful enough to live in style in Thailand for the rest of your life, and the other means you'll need occasionally work to support your travel habit. No judgment on either, but it should be obvious from this example that goals make a huge difference in where you end up — but only if you make them and then work towards them.

#94: Solve the Problem of How to Solve The Problem

I've found over the years that understanding how to solve a problem is far more important than solving it.

Huh?

Heuristics are techniques I can apply to any problem to improve my chances of solving it. Not every one of course, but I can reduce the churn by zeroing in on some specific methods:

• Sleep on it. When all else fails, think about the problem before beddy-bye, and then sleep. Sometimes — sometimes — I've woken up with an answer.

• Let your subconscious take over. Sleep is one example. Doing other work, like getting immersed in something radically different can help. Do you draw? Do you play video games? (I'm kidding — everyone plays video games!) I once had a thorny problem without a solution. After a lot of fruitless thinking, I finally left work and headed home. Part way there the answer popped into my head. Just about any distraction, once you've loaded the whole problem in your brain, seems to work.

• Ask for assistance. Find people that help you answer problems. My wife is invaluable in this regard (and many, many more of course!) She is a tireless sounding board when I have an issue, and often just explaining it to her helps immensely. Plus, since she's not in the tech field, I get practice converting technobabble to normal peoplespeak, which also helps me to analyze and review the problem.

• Recognize that there are bad days for problem solving. We all have them, where we bump into walls, or pause a full three seconds when replying to people. Those are also bad days to do detailed coding. Guaranteed, you WILL pay for trying to code on a bad day. So can you do some other necessary task that doesn't tax the brain as much? Obviously, you can't avoid coding for too long, but doing the wrong thing on a bad day isn't a time saver: You'll waste more time reworking or replacing that code when you get clear-headed again. Bad code has come back and plagued me on so many occasions when I said it just had to be done right now. Don't let it plague you.

• Ask what works for others. Who knows, someone may have a solution for what ails you. Read magazines and books on algorithms to keep the brain primed with solutions. But don't limit yourself to just computer problems and solutions: I was once extremely tired while doing my job — my boss noticed, and mentioned a specialty diet. I tried it, had great success, and that launched me on a search for better health regimes. Oh, and with less fatigue, my programming got better (I mean, "even better!")

• Test out what works for you. This is just a quick sampler of ways to solve problems. There are even more out there. Some work for one person, but not for another. Try what sounds good, pay attention to how well it works, and focus on the ones that do. Ultimately, life is one very long (if you're fortunate) series of hacks, figuring out how to solve any problem in life, not just computer-related. So keep alert to what works for you, whether or not it does for someone else. As they say, results may vary.

#95: Embrace the Itch

Do you have "the itch" (no, no, not that one)? Great programmers have them. Like great artists, they see the whole picture, and have an overpowering urge or craving or itch to make it "right" – not necessarily perfect (which is impossible) but well crafted, even elegant.

Take an example of changing the background color on a screen. A regular programmer likely won't care what the background is, and program whatever is specified. A good programmer mulls over the code and says I think it will look better with a different color, more visually pleasing. Both are perfectly fine responses.

But a great programmer will go beyond one screen; perhaps it would involve developing an entire palette of colors for the display, all visually balanced and lovely, and then double down by reworking the program to use multiple color themes. And quite likely, all this in a single weekend or even overnight. Now, a little itch about the display has turned into a truly marketable feature (who doesn't like themes?)

Balance of course is necessary. Just like some artists had to paint portraits to make a living, sometimes you'll just have to grit your teeth and code SQL statements. But when you do get a chance, do the assigned work, and then try to do above and beyond that. When and where allowed, of course; fighting with the boss when you "know" your idea is better is a sure way to not have a boss (and may explain why many great programmers are self-employed.)

Programmers can be artists. An amateur throws paint at a canvas hoping something good comes out. But a real artist can look at a painting and know how to improve it with a brushstroke, by repainting large sections, or sometimes redoing the whole painting. And just as that level of skill requires effort for an artist, so too with programmers. With experience, training and practice you'll eventually just look at code you wrote and know where it can be improved. A line here, an adjustment there, and it looks better, works better, IS better. And more importantly, you will want to do that again and again, because sending out code that hasn't been tweaked properly will feel wrong, unfinished.

The result? Eventually, your itch for quality will get you noticed. In the first tip of this book, I quoted Proverbs, talking about how a "truly competent" worker will serve kings rather than the ordinary people. Really good programmers will always be in demand. So follow that itch, care about your software, and you will get great.

#96: ...And One Other Thing...

Here it is — the last one. Simple really.

Never stop learning:

• Read voraciously. And if you don't know what "voraciously" means, look it up, and begin your reading journey with adding that to your vocabulary (and even if you think you know it, look it up and confirm you do — go ahead, I'll wait).

• Learn from the past. Read about software mistakes, programmer's viewpoints and observations about their programming, and then ask yourself how good coding could have prevented it. Then become that coder.

• Understand your favorite language's nook and crannies. Read the docs, and the latest books on your language. Or languages, if you deal in more than one. As you learn the rules, you'll get more confident applying them — and your code will reflect your confidence.

• Grab education. One of my first jobs offered free tuition for related programming courses. To this day, I regret being too young and stupid not to make more use of it. If that's an option for you, remember that low-cost or no-cost education is always a bargain.

• Stretch. Challenge yourself to new jobs and opportunities. Avoid stagnation by looking for new ways to improve yourself. Learn new languages. Try different philosophies of programming (like functional programming) and force yourself to work with new devices, techniques, algorithms, and anything else you can find to expand your experience. Be the person they come to when they need something never before seen — and be the person that can successfully deliver it.

• Simply put, never stop. Always seek out more and better, and learn to be the best programmer you can be. It's a challenge, but you're up to it — after all, you got through this book, didn't you?

Conclusion

As with the introduction to this book, I wonder who reads these parts. Don't worry, there's nothing much here — you're excused.

Well, OK, one last bit of advice. Quit reading, go out now and apply whatever you want from this book into your life.

And strive to become a better programmer.

A Professional Programmer.

About the Author

Like the other "expected" parts of books, I've never quite got what the "About the Author" section was for. You've just read a whole book chock-full of my thoughts; so what else is left to talk about? I'm just not that interesting (I wish I were, but I'm not).

However, if you absolutely need more, then visit my blog at

www.UtopiaMechanicus.com

Finally, if you're like me and have to read to the very end to feel you've "read" the book, I now absolve you: Put the book down, you're done!